I Gotta Be Me

I Gotta Be Me

by Tammy Bakker
with Cliff Dudley

NEW LEAF PRESS

Harrison, Arkansas 72601

Library of Congress Catalog Card Number: 78-64670

First Printing, December 1978
Second Printing, February 1979
Third Printing, April 1979
Fourth Printing, July 1979
Fifth Printing, September 1979
Sixth Printing, February 1980

International Standard Book Number: 0-89221-48-6

CONTENTS

PREFACE

After I had told Jim Bakker that I would write his wife's book, I started having second thoughts. What would sweet little Tammy Faye Bakker have to say about anything.

John Utterback, the pilot who flew me to PTL, went to her office with me for the first taping session. Just as we were to enter her office, I turned to John and said, "Be prepared for a plastic world."

For the first hour or so of the taping it was as I had expected, little or nothing. Then with the suddenness of a summer storm, Tammy started telling it all! People, places, dates, hurts . . . everything. My first reaction was, this is too hot to handle. But the Lord very clearly spoke and said, "This is of Me."

This cute little blond turned into a woman of great strength and spiritual depth. The taping of her book soon became one of the spiritual highlights of my life as we prayed, laughed and cried together.

I'VE GOTTA BE ME is bold and daring. What Tammy Faye has said has been needed for years, but no one has had the courage. I believe time will reveal this to be one of the top books of this decade.

—Cliff Dudley

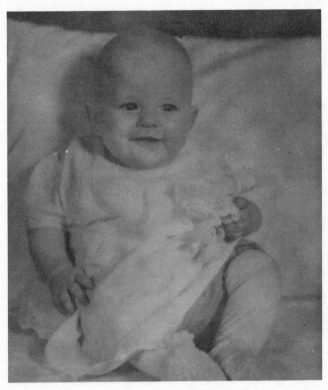

Tamara Faye La Valley

FOREWORD

Hello, Hello, Hello,

Not being a professional writer in the journalistic area, I felt very backward when they asked me to come forward to write this foreword. In other words, as a songwriter, I feel very comfortable about being forward. But, as a journalist, I feel very backward about this foreword. Then I prayed about it and the Lord said, "Gary S., Tammy and Jim have done so much for you in bringing you out of your fear of being on T.V. and out in front of people, that it is wrong to be backward about this foreword." So, I came forward to write this foreword. I pray that this foreword doesn't cause this book to go backward. Now that you understand all of this clearly, I will tell you about this book:

Number 1. I haven't read it, but I know it's great! I asked for a copy so I could write this foreword and say something about the book; however, they couldn't find a copy for me and they said, "Go buy one when it comes out." So, I'll tell you about the nut the book is about by answering some of the many questions people all over the country ask me about her.

A lot of people ask, "Is Tammy really that short?" My answer is, "No, she just gets caught standing in a hole every time they take her picture and, on top of that, she's only a little short on one end, not on both ends." Then they ask, "Does she giggle and yakketity-yak all the time, like we see her on T.V.?" The answer is, "~~No,~~ YES. Most people don't know but Tammy was a special nurse that was hired on many occasions to keep people (who had acute sleeping sickness) awake." Many others ask me,

9

"What's she really like in person; is she the same behind the scenes as in front of the camera?" I say, "Definitely, she still has hair, two ears, two eyes; she giggles; she cries; she loves Jesus; she worships God; she loves and takes good care of Jim, Tammy Sue, and Jamie Charles as a devoted wife and mother." Others ask, "Is she a good driver?" On that, I say, "If you ever see her or my wife, Karen, either separately or especially together, slow down, move over to the right and let them pass! They both have enough fuzz between their ears to cover a basketball ten feet in diameter."

Last but not least, they ask if she has a moustache. The answer is, "No. The moustache she wears sometimes is definitely phony."

I hope all of this has truly enlightened you. I know it did me when I read it back.

Now, it's your turn to come forward and, after you've read this backward foreword, read this forward book about a wonderful LADY we all love very deeply for being just what you see on T.V., 24 hours a day.

Don't change, Tammy, we couldn't go through all this again. We all love you!

Yours in Christ,
Gary S. Paxton

Chapter 1

EARLY INFLUENCE

Jim slowly pulled the car to the curb, turned the motor off and looked at me for a moment with his eyes saying, "Tammy, it will be all right."

Often, after I married Jim, he would talk to me about my real father. I told what I knew about my father, and how I was so frightened of him.

Jim felt I should meet him for my own peace of mind, and also to satisfy my natural curiosity. "He is your real father, and I think you should see him," Jim told me.

Now here Jim and I were in International Falls. I had called Aunt Dolly, Dad's twin sister, and she said, "Tammy, your dad is over here now. Would you please come over and meet him?"

"Tammy, now is the time," Jim said.

Fear gripped me as I saw Jim coming around the car to open the door. My legs turned to concrete. My feet were as stone. I could not move. My mind raced through the years and then I heard the door click. I thought, "Why, why did I let Jim talk me into this? I have kept this moment out of my mind for over twenty years, and now I am exposing myself to more hurt."

I looked at Jim and said, "Jim, please let's go." As

these words came from my lips, I looked up and saw four men standing in front of the small house where we had just parked the car. My eyes became like searchlights as I went from the left to the right—from the right to the left. "Which one?" I thought, "Which one?" They stood there not moving, nor did I.

Jim broke the eerie silence when he said, "Come on, Tammy. Come on. Let's get it over with."

Slowly I put one leg out of the car and tried to force the other to follow. Again, my eyes searched, trying to decide, "Which one? Which one?" I thought I couldn't stand the pressure anymore when the youngest-looking of the four men stepped forward. His voice sounded like lightning cracking through gray clouds as he said, "Tammy Faye, I'm your daddy!" I was surprised. I thought he'd be older.

As I looked into the eyes of the stranger whom I did not recognize and heard the words, "I'm your daddy," I thought to myself, "My daddy, how could you be my daddy? I don't know you! You have never held me in your arms. You have never cared for me! Daddy? You are not my daddy! You are simply a man I am meeting for the first time in my life."

Then he stepped forward and gave me a kiss, and as he kissed me it was as though sirens and skyrockets went off in my mind. I could hardly handle it. *Why did he do that? Why? Who am I to him?*

We made some small talk and met the others who were standing there. They were uncles I scarcely knew. I stood at a loss for words and actions. I didn't know whether to lift one arm or the other, to move forward or backward, to run or to scream. I couldn't blot out the memories. I couldn't help thinking, "Oh, if you only knew. If you only knew!"

As I stood there my mind went back to the day that all my fear and fright began. I was only three years old at the time but I've never forgotten that moment. The scene was so vivid in my mind. I heard my mother screaming. In the shadows I saw my father and he was yelling at my mother. I realized that something was terribly wrong. Now as I stood looking at that man who was calling me his daughter, I cried, "Oh, Jesus, help me to forgive. Help me to forget. I know he can never be my daddy for my real daddy is the one who has raised me all these years. Help me, Lord. Help me to forgive him."

* * * * *

Once again I heard the screams of my mother and then there was silence. The door had closed. My father was gone and our lives were going to change abruptly. And they did. I soon, as a child, would know the meaning of the word "divorce."

My mother and dad divorced shortly after that. This left my mother with two children, Donny and me. From that time on I was always afraid of my father, and until adulthood I didn't want to see him.

In a few years my mother remarried a wonderful man whom I love dearly and was to me my daddy. Even though there were eight of us children in the family we always had clothes and food. We weren't rich. As a matter of fact, our family was almost poor. All during my childhood we only had an outside privy (bathroom).

When I was only three months old I started having convulsions. Without warning they would hit me with a fury and each time they seemed to get worse. It was very rare that my mother ever called a doctor. The first thing she would do was to call the pastor of our Assembly of God Church to come and pray. The pastor had dedicated me to the Lord, so he had a very special concern for me. One day the convulsions were so bad that mother called him to come to the house and pray. He came and anointed me with oil and prayed in faith believing. He then turned to Mother and said, "Mrs. LaValley, the devil might try and return with another convulsion, but Tammy Faye has been healed by the power of God. If the devil comes back you simply put your hand on her head and say the name of Jesus three times."

In a few days I went into another convulsion. My eyes began to roll, and I started to swallow my tongue. Mother simply placed her hand on my head and whispered, "Jesus, Jesus, Jesus!" At once I responded, and to this day I have never had another convulsion. God completely healed me. What power there is in the name of Jesus!

I recall clearly my first day at school. Mother stood me on a chair and got me dressed in a real fluffy dress. I went to school and loved it with all my heart. It was just wonderful. Maybe it was the walk to school and Mrs. Ness's Store. All of us kids would stop there and spend most of our lunch money. It was also a cozy place to warm up on cold days.

I got my first taste of the world and its disappointments in the second grade. My teacher accused me of plugging up the sink in the girls' restroom with a brown paper towel. I told her I didn't do it, but she wouldn't believe me. That bothered me for years that she thought I would plug up that sink and even tell a lie, when I didn't do it. One of the other girls had done it and blamed me. For years I felt the shame of that moment. I knew I was innocent but couldn't prove it!

Music has always been a very important part of my life and I would always be singing in school. Every free moment I would sing, "Jesus Loves Me." One day on the playground almost every kid in the school followed me around. Can you imagine 100 kids following me in a big, long line and all singing, "Jesus Loves Me?" I have been singing for Jesus ever since.

I'm the oldest of eight kids and always remember us in this order: Tammy, Donny, Larry, Judy, Danny, Johnny, Debbie and Ruth. I was the baby-sitter for everybody. As each child came along we would be waiting by the telephone to hear what it was. I always thought babies were only born after midnight, in the middle of the night. Mother had very difficult deliveries. Knowing about her difficult childbirths frightened me very much regarding bearing children in later years. Generally speaking, I was a happy-go-lucky girl.

There have been various people in my life who have been very important to me. One was my Aunt Virginia Fairchild (Aunt Gin). She was like my second mother. Mom was always so busy with all the other kids and everything else that she had to do so it was hard for her to pay special attention to each of us. However, we all felt very much loved. I would never have had a chance to eat out unless I had gone with Aunt Gin. Mother, rather than take all eight of us kids to some eating place, thought it was easier to eat at home.

Because I was the oldest I did a lot of baby-sitting. Every Saturday Mother would give me a choice. I could clean the house or take the kids to the playground so that she could clean the house. Most of the time I'd take the kids to the playground and let Mom clean the house. I felt I had raised about half of the kids.

My special fun times were with Aunt Gin. She would make me frilly dresses and would take me with her to places I would never have gone otherwise. I would go to her house and take a bath in her tub. Aunt Gin would give me permanents, fix my hair, and taught me about the graces that a lady should know. The thing Aunt Gin tried to teach me that never took was not to speak too loudly.

We lived in International Falls, Minnesota. I thought

our house was huge until I got married and discovered how little the house really was. But to me it was the biggest house in the whole world. When I think about it now there were only four bedrooms in the house—three of them upstairs and one downstairs. Our house had a small living room and a small dining room that connected, and a kitchen. The living room had a big Junger's oil stove in it, like right in the middle so it would keep both rooms warm. We had a back porch with windows all around it and a little porch on the front of the house.

Saturday nights at our house was just a riot because that was when we got our baths. Mother would heat the water on the stove in great big kettles. We'd bring in this large, round galvanized tub and put it by the stove and let it warm up. Mother then would take the hot water from the stove and fill the tub. She'd bathe the little kids in the sink. Then us big ones in the tub. The cleanest ones got in first. The little ones hated for us big ones to be taking a bath when they were taking a bath because they didn't want us looking at them. I recall hearing, "Mama, make her get out of here. Make her get out." While we were bathing Mother would put a big pot of fudge on the stove and go to the radio and turn on the Saturday night "Barn Dance."

While the fudge was cooking, one at a time, we'd get our baths. Then, one by one we'd sit on the couch and wait for the other kids to be bathed, and for the fudge to get done. We all had to take a bath in that one tub and with the same water.

The ones not sitting on the couch were sitting on chairs, or on the floor. Then Mother would give each a great big hunk of fudge. She made the best fudge in the whole world! I can still almost taste it.

After we ate she would take us upstairs and sing to us. Bedtime was such a wonderful time. We would all be in our beds and Mother would be rocking the littlest one by our beds. There were three or four of us in a bed sometimes. Mother would sing real sad songs as we went to sleep. Most of the songs were about little children or puppies going to heaven, or something like that. As a result, most of us would fall asleep bawling our eyes out.

Mother has always been a very tender-hearted woman. When she was a little girl she was called to the mission field, but instead of obeying God, she married my dad, who was an unsaved man.

Mother is an exceptionally good singer. She has such a beautiful voice and many other talents. It always hurt my heart that she never did something full time for the Lord. She prayed that God would let me do the work that she had never done. That was real special to me because she'd say, "Lord, help Tammy some day to be able to win the souls that I was never able to win."

The divorce almost destroyed my mother. Even after she remarried she was not real happy. My step-father did some things that Mother didn't like. He drank. He didn't drink and get drunk, he just drank and got happy. He also smoked. Mother had never been around people who smoked, and that constantly bothered her. I never once remember my father smoking in the house. My mother would never have allowed it! She never allowed anyone to smoke in our house. She always asked them to please step outside, even in the coldest weather.

My step-father was good and very kind to all of us. He was a very gentle man, but in some ways he also appeared to be very stern and harsh. Donny and I were his step-children. He and mother had six of their own. People were always trying to tell Donny and me that he was treating us differently because we were not his, but he didn't. That was a real source of hurt because I really loved my daddy. I always felt I could never hug and kiss my step-

17

Back row: Judy, Tammy, Donny, and Larry
Front row: Danny and Johnny

Me and Aunt Gin, I have on a dress she made me.

father. I don't know why I felt this way. Maybe it is something inborn in a little girl. Something that says it is not proper. How I longed to sit on daddy's lap and be hugged and kissed like other little girls were.

About the only time I ever had a feeling of his partiality was the time Donny and Larry threw a hammer at our pet duck and crippled it. When Dad came home from work he beat the boys with a belt until he drew blood on their backs. To this day I can see my mother, tears streaming down her face, wiping the blood off my brothers' backs, and my father hating himself for beating them like he did. Deep down I thought that he had beaten Donny harder than Larry.

Donny and I were very close. The other kids came along so quickly that everyone fit in real good. Most of us are only two years apart, just like stairsteps. It wasn't until years later that I knew, or realized, that Donny and I were brother and sister and not half brother and sister. But I have never considered any of us as half and always get aggravated if anyone mentions the word half . . . we are all brothers and sisters.

We were all very secure as children. I think that's why I never wanted to see my real father because I was afraid he would break up my security.

Having Daddy come home at night was something exciting for us kids, because his lunch pail almost always carried a little surprise for us. We would all race to see who could get the lunch box first. Every now and then there would be a candy bar, or an apple. Those were the very special days.

One day Mother said to me, "Tammy, I have a surprise for you, honey. From now on you can have your own room!" With so many kids at home I had never dreamed I could have my own room. I ran upstairs to the room and I just stared and cried. The room was like an attic room. It

19

came down real steep on one side. Mom had white ruffled curtains on the windows and a white bedspread on my bed. That was the greatest thing in the whole world to me—that I could have my own bed, with my own room! I placed a little plaque over my bed: "God Cares." It glowed in the dark. I couldn't go to sleep without looking at that plaque. Praise God, He still cares.

One time I wanted to redecorate my room. My stepfather worked at one of the largest wood pulp mills in the world and could buy things real cheap, so we always had lots of scrap paper around the house. One day he brought home a stack of wrapping paper so I decided I was going to "wall paper" my room. I took straight pins and stuck hundreds of pieces of wrapping paper all over my room. That was my first decorating venture. I've loved to decorate ever since.

Mother raised all of us children to think of and call upon God in every situation. During the summer in International Falls thunderstorms were the norm, but that never made me get used to them.

Whenever it would storm mother would gather all of us children into the living room and we would pray and sing. She would tell us not to be afraid, that Jesus rides on the wings of the storm. One of the storms I remember most vividly was a very severe lightning storm. We could all look out the window and see the trees bending under the wind, and streak after streak of lightning dance across the late afternoon sky. Then we saw it! A ball of fire! It must have been at least three feet in diameter and it was heading for our house. Our hearts almost stopped. Just then that big ball of fire came down, balanced on top of the telephone pole in front of our house, went around and around the pole all the way to the ground. It knocked out every bit of electricity in the entire area. Praise the Lord, He is the God of the Universe.

There was never a dull moment around our house. Someone was always getting into something or other. One time I was in my closet trying to change a light bulb when a surge of power went through me and I thought I was going to die. I began to shake and I couldn't for the life of me stop. I was afraid to run to mother in fear that I would die right there in front of her. I wonder how mothers ever survive.

Mother loved each of us equally and always had time to sit and talk to us. When we got home from school she had a big supper fixed. One of her greatest meals was meatballs, gravy and mashed potatoes. Her grocery list was something like this:

10 loaves bread
12 to 15 quarts milk
10 cans peas
10 cans corn
10 cans tomatoes, etc. (She'd buy 10 cans of everything.)

After I was married I'd buy 10 cans of things and Jim would just laugh himself sick—me buying all those groceries for the two of us! But I didn't know how to buy any other way. I also had trouble scaling the menus down because that was also the way I learned to cook. Even my small meals would last Jim and me a whole week.

When Mother would go shopping I would sit home and watch the kids. Almost everytime she shopped there would be something for each of us, even if it only cost a nickel. Little trucks for the boys, paper dolls and coloring books for the girls.

Mother always made Christmas extraordinary. Daddy and the boys would go to the woods trudging through the snow and chop down our Christmas tree. Christmas Eve the tree was filled with an enormous amount of toys. I'm sure Mother paid for them the rest of the year! We would get crepe paper, cut it into strips and decorate the whole house. What wonderful memories!

Grandma and Grandpa Fairchild's house was very special to me. Grandma was my very best friend. Gram raised birds. One whole room in their house was a big bird cage. Grandma had a parrot named Polly, and it seemed hundreds of parakeets and canaries. She raised them for the local stores to sell.

When our school class went for a walk I would bring them to her house so we could see how baby birds were hatched and raised. That parrot was sure a mean one. She really wasn't, but I was scared to death of her. She would just talk and holler at us for hours. This trip was the thrill of the year for most of the children. Of course, it made me feel great because it was my grandma!

Spending the night at Grandma's was the greatest. She had a record player and I would play record after record and sing along at the top of my voice. Every few minutes— 15 to be exact—the large grandfather clock in the hall would chime, trying to drown me out. I loved to sit in her rocking chair that squeaked every time you went back and forth. Grandma let me comb her long, long gray hair by the hour.

Sometimes Grandma would let Polly out of the cage and that parrot would chase me all over the house . . . me screaming up a storm, "Grandma, help! Polly's after me!" and jumping up on Grandma's white bedspread. Grandma would come in just laughing and laughing because she knew Polly wouldn't hurt me, but I didn't know it. I used to have nightmares about that dumb bird catching me!

Often while baby-sitting we would become terrified if we heard a strange noise. Once I looked out the window and saw a man standing under the large crab-apple tree in our back yard. I sent Donny to get all the kitchen knives in the house and put them by the back door. I quickly put a pot of water to boil on the stove so if he came in I'd stab him with a knife and throw hot water on him. I was only four feet tall at the time but I really felt brave. My father had this large knife that looked like a pirates' knife. I got it ready too just in case, but the man disappeared. He was probably someone we knew! Would he have gotten a surprise if he'd knocked on the door.

Sometimes when I would baby-sit my brothers and sisters would get mean and I'd chase them outside with a broom in zero weather and tell them if they didn't behave I was going to make them stay out there. I don't know how we all survived.

With eight children there were lots of accidents around our house. One of my brothers had a little toy fire engine, the kind you sit on and ride. The steering wheel came off and left a rod poker-like sticking up. One day he fell on it and poked the rod down his throat. We had to rush him to the hospital.

One day my sister let me wipe the dishes. I dropped one, fell and cut open my leg. My dad just pushed the wound back together and put on lots of bandages. To this day I still have that scar on my right leg.

We seldom went to doctors at our house. I never had a vaccination or a shot until after I was married. We just believed God would heal us and take care of us. That was pushed into my mind, that God was able to do anything. Nothing was too hard for the Lord. As a result, we were hardly ever sick.

Chapter 2

LEARNING TO LEAN

Daddy had this old Model A Ford that he was always painting in different colors. That car was just awful to me. I walked to work every day, even in 40 degrees below weather. It was a mile and a half one way. So that was a three-mile walk every day. I think that's what kept me at 73 pounds. Sometimes I would call and ask Daddy to come and get me. He would always talk to that car like it was alive: "Come on now. Get up there, Maggie. Let's go." All the way home I would hope no one would see me.

Speech class in school was one of my favorite subjects. I was good at making speeches. I could make up a speech on the spur of the moment. Everybody else would have to take their lessons home and work on them into the night. Me, I'd sit there in class and when others were giving their speeches I would make up one, I would do "how to" speeches: how to sew, how to do this or that, because I loved to work with my hands.

One of the highlights of my life was that I was in the choir at school. I was a contralto. Our choir would travel and we would go places where we would enter competitions. Our choir won often.

I was selected for a part in the play "Oklahoma," and

it really meant a lot to me. However, I had inner conflict over these plays because I had always been taught they were wrong. However, I was starting to sort out things for myself a little better. I was beginning to step out and do some things and be a bit liberated from that strict code of the church. Our church was a "Can't Do Church." You can't do this, and you can't do that! We weren't allowed to wear slacks except if we were ice skating. Most of my awakening on these things came after I was married. A good start for me was singing in that play. I thought I was very brave to even be in the play at all because I had turned down everything until that time.

I was very embarrassed about sex in front of mother. As a matter of fact, I was very embarrassed about sex, period. I started to get nervous about sex at about age 15, after I started dating. I got to thinking about how people got pregnant. I couldn't figure it out for the life of me, and I didn't dare ask anybody.

I didn't even tell my mother when I bought my first bra. I was on my way home from school and noticed someone having a garage sale. I found there this old, faded, light-blue bra, perhaps a 30. My heart was pounding fifteen miles an hour as I took it from the rack. I paid twenty cents for it. I ran home and sneaked upstairs to my room and put the bra on. It was too big. I was very embarrassed in gym class that I still wasn't wearing a bra in the seventh grade. The other girls were all wearing bras. I stuffed some kleenex in the bra and went downstairs to set the table. I felt like Marilyn Monroe, 40-D, but I was all of 30. I was so afraid that my mother wasn't going to notice that there was something different about me and also afraid that she would. Then I thought, she will surely notice that I have blossomed. She never said a word about it, and I never said a word about it to her. I just never had the courage to talk to Mother about stuff like that.

I knew I had to know about sex because a boy had kissed me. And, oh, Lord, I thought I was pregnant. I summoned all the courage I could muster and went to mother who was standing and peeling potatoes at the sink. I said, "Mama, can I talk to you?"

"Sure, honey."

"If a boy kisses you, can you get pregnant?"

She should have told me "yes," but she said, "No, honey, you can't get pregnant from just a boy kissing you." Then she explained how a woman gets pregnant. I couldn't believe what I was hearing. After that my girl friend and I decided we'd better read some books on sex. As we read we just laughed and laughed, and vowed "no boys are ever going to get near us."

God began to speak to me that He is a God of love. Our pastor had begun to teach about a God of love and that He isn't a God that's looking down with a big stick in hand, and ready to clobber you everytime you did something. The first time I wore make-up was in that play. I had been taught if you put on lipstick you are going to hell. That was it! How thankful I was that by now I had learned that God really loved me.

One Sunday afternoon I was at my girl friend's house. Ada DeRadd had gotten some make-up at the store for twenty cents. She was putting on some eye make-up when I asked, "Ada, do you think I dare try?"

She was pushing me with, "Yeah, Tammy, try it!"

I decided I would put some on my eye lashes, and when I did I realized I had super long eye lashes and that I looked prettier with eye make-up. Then I knew that it had to be wrong and of the devil. It scared me when I first saw make-up on me. I took it right off and said, "Oh, I can't do this! I can't do this!" Then I thought, "Why can't I do this? If it makes me look prettier, why can't I do this?" So I began to wear make-up. Just eye make-up. The kids on the church bus saw it and talked about my eyes, but I didn't care. I was very close to the Lord and felt that God would speak to me in my heart if I really shouldn't wear it. I felt what I did at home I would do at church. I never did wear lipstick until after I was married. I was very, very careful about my testimony. I wanted to live my testimony. When I did wear the make-up I didn't feel condemned. I began to wonder if maybe there wasn't more to serving the Lord than I thought. I discovered that God was more open than I had realized. I searched the Bible and read books, always searching for truth. Way down deep in my heart I felt many of the people at our church had been old fuddy-duddies on such things and that there was a place of liberation with the Lord.

One time my mother and father were going to see the movie "The Ten Commandments." I told mother if she went to that movie I'd leave home and never return. I thought I would keep her from backsliding. They went, and I cried and cried. I saw my very first movie after I was married. I'll never forget it. It was "White Christmas," with Bing Crosby.

In the winter time it was often too cold to go to the outdoor bathroom. So Daddy brought home a big twenty-gallon pail that we used. He'd put it on the porch. That was the bathroom. It was cold on the porch, but not as cold as going outside. He brought home a smaller pail for us to take upstairs in case us kids had to go to the bathroom in the middle of the night. Mama had told us we were to empty that pail every day. The boys had gone for two days without emptying it. Mother kept saying, "Boys, I told you to empty that pail, now do it!"

"I'm going to, I'm going to," Donny said. But he never did.

One of my little brothers decided he would be sweet to Mom and would empty the pail. Just as he got to the stairway he tripped and the pail—two days' worth—went all down the stairs. It leaked through the stairs into a closet that Dad had built under the stairs, and all over the clothes. You can not imagine poor Mother having to clean up that terrible, terrible mess. You can't imagine what the boys got, and you can bet they always emptied the pail after that. Every day!

Youth camp was very special to me. Especially during my early teens. Those were the years I wanted to be popular in school. But because of my "standards" for Jesus, couldn't date most of the boys. However, when I went to youth camp my popularity would climb to the top and I would be the "belle of the ball." Two years in a row I was chosen "Queen" of the Bible camp. That was a vote amongst all for the most popular girl at camp.

During those years I would spend hours at the altars. I prayed much when I was young. I would spend hours seeking God. It was more important to me than anything in the whole world. The only thing that kept me was the baptism in the Holy Spirit. Youth Camp was a time when all of us teenagers from our church would go and be refreshed by the Lord.

At this time I was thinking more about my real father, but only because I wanted to know what he looked like. I didn't know who I looked like and I was inquisitive. I was asking Mother some questions about him. She showed me some pictures. Mother never talked about him unless I asked her, and then she was very open. I was becoming aware that I had other relatives that I didn't know. From photos I realized they were totally different-looking people than any of the people I was living with. I was interested in knowing my roots. Mother told me my real father was French.

Now that I am raising two children and sometimes come to my wits end, I realize that eight kids must have almost driven Mom out of her mind. Also, Daddy wasn't the type of person to come home and help. He would come home, read the paper and sit. Of course, he had worked hard all day and was tired. I wish I would have known then what I know now and what it was like to raise children. I wouldn't have complained so much. So many times I have wished I could go back for one twenty-four hour day and give Mom a day off.

Dad often helped me with my homework. He must have written my "times tables" a hundred times for me.

One cold winter day something wonderful happened at our house. Daddy came home and as usual we all ran for his lunch pail, but he told us all to stand still a minute and he pulled out from under his big overcoat a tiny, black fuzzy puppy. Us kids about went crazy. We named him Smokey. We put him in front of the stove to get him warm and all played with him. Mom wouldn't have the dog in the house so Smokey had to stay out on the porch. Smokey living with us gave me a love for animals. There was an ordinance in our city that dogs couldn't run free so the dog had to be tied up all of the time. We kept him on a long chain. We had him about ten years, and, of course, he grew from a puppy to a big dog. He was a good friend to all of us children.

One hot day some kids came into our yard and a little boy knocked Smokey's water over. As a result Smokey bit the boy on the cheek. Mom sent us to the playground and then called my uncle who came and shot Smokey. When we got home we looked and looked for Smokey. We found him in the garbage can. I thought I would die with grief. Part of my "life" seemed to be in that garbage can. How could Mother do such a thing? Why? I questioned.

That night we had a funeral for Smokey. My dad buried him in the back yard in the garden, with tears streaming down his cheeks. We all cried and cried. Mother had him shot because she was afraid it would cause trouble. She had also heard that once a dog had the taste of blood he would bite again. I still feel sad when I think of Smokey. Perhaps that is the reason I've had as many as three dogs, and five birds at a time. Sometimes Jim feels he lives in an animal shelter. But I feel a home is not a home without pets around. Every little child needs a pet.

Grandma and Grandpa Fairchild

Chapter 3

THE CHURCH AND MOM

I was in church every Sunday. I didn't go to the same church my Mother attended. I went to the Mission Covenant Church. This group did not believe in the baptism of the Holy Spirit, or, at least it was never preached. They just believed in salvation. I went there with Aunt Gin until I was ten years old. I wouldn't go to my parents' church because I heard they did strange things. I was now too "proper" to go to the Pentecostal Church and do "wild things." Every Sunday Aunt Gin would take me to church, then we would go out to eat.

When I was ten years old I became acquainted with a girl named Marion Kasara. One day she asked, "Tammy, would you like to go to church with me?"

I thought, *Boy, this is going to be a really big step for me to go to church with Marion!* "Yes, Marion," I answered, "I will go to the Tuesday night prayer meeting with you." I had heard about the things they did at that church as I had visited one other time. I had seen the kids at the altar. They seemed so happy and God meant so much to them. Deep in my heart I wanted something.

All these years I'd been going to church but I had never asked Jesus to come into my heart. I thought going to church automatically made me a Christian. I knew that those kids who went to the altar had something, but I didn't know what it was. I went to prayer meeting that night with Marion. That was the night that changed my entire life.

Marion's church was also where my mother attended. I could not wait for the preacher to finish with his sermon, something was happening inside of me. I almost ran up to the first row of seats and knelt down when he finished and the altar call was given. As I did so I said, *"Jesus, come into my heart and forgive me of my sins. I don't know what this is that everybody is getting, but if it is real, and it is for me, please Jesus, give that to me."* I began to cry.

Then I saw myself in a picture as the tallest person in the whole world. Then slowly, slowly, slowly, I came down and I disappeared and the Lord filled me with His Holy Spirit. For hours I lay on the floor and spoke in an unknown language. I wasn't aware of anyone else. I was walking with Jesus. The church people left and when I opened my eyes my Mom was there. Someone had gone to our house and had brought her to church. From that day forward I went to the Assembly of God Church.

A week later I still felt I was three feet off the ground. I just couldn't get my feet down to earth. I wanted to tell everybody about Jesus and what He had done for me. I wanted to tell how wonderful He is and what He could do for them. Jesus and the church now became my life. Whenever I was asked what I wanted to be I'd always say, "I want to be an evangelist missionary." I loved Jesus. I served Him. I talked to Him. He was my whole life.

I enjoyed going to the same church as Mom and my brothers and sisters. We had wonderful, wonderful old-fashioned pentecostal services in those days. I'll never forget the sight of my precious little brothers and sisters kneeling at the altars, their little hands raised, tears streaming down their little faces, saying, "Jesus, Jesus, Jesus."

Then I wondered what I would tell Aunt Gin. This church had just what I was looking for and I knew that I would now attend there with my mother. When I told Aunt Gin what Jesus had done for me she was really happy for me. It wasn't long until I would go home with some of the kids from church to their house rather than to always go to Grandma's house with Aunt Gin. I think she knew there was coming a time when I couldn't be just her little girl any longer.

There was also a little jealousy starting between the other kids at home and me, because Aunt Gin was giving me things that the others were not getting.

The first time I ever sang in a tent meeting was at an A. A. Allen Evangelistic Crusade. I was so small Mr. Allen would pick me up and put me on a chair in front of the microphone. (We had never had a ride on a bus, so when Mom took us by bus I was excited about that.) Those were the days when the power of the Lord moved and we saw many people healed. Those were also the days of the scoffers, when it wasn't popular to be a Spirit-filled Christian. The scoffers would stand around the outside of the tent and poke fun at us, laugh, and shout, "Holy Rollers." We took our share of deep criticism for being Spirit-filled.

It was a very hard thing for me to cope with the way the people at the church treated my mother. It was also very hard for me to share. I loved my mother so much. I was very young when I became aware that the church people were being mean to my mother. I couldn't figure out why. They would let me do everything in church but they wouldn't let Mom do anything. All the pastors liked my Mom because she was so outgoing and talented, but the pastors' wives would soon get jealous of my mother. The women in the church too were jealous of Mom because she could do what they couldn't do.

My Mom was the type to invite the whole church over after services, even all the kids. She would spend all day making fancy sandwiches and all sorts of goodies. After eating they would sit around and she'd play the piano and everyone would sing. I couldn't understand how the church people could come and eat, take advantage of all the things she did for them and then treat her like they did. This hurt me so deeply, and there was almost an undercurrent of hate in me toward those church people. Many a Sunday I would hear Mother cry and cry. I'd cry also because this hurt me so.

My step-father didn't go to church with us so Mother had to face it alone. Mom was the kind of person who would give her very last $30 in the offering because the church had a need, and they knew she gave it. I couldn't understand how they could take her money but wouldn't even let her play the piano. The people would speak in tongues and act so saintly and holy in church and yet treated my mother so terrible. I never understood this, but I knew I had a Jesus that was able to cover all of this. I thanked God that He kept my heart tender.

Our church fell apart twice and closed its doors. It seemed everybody in the church was vying for power. It was—Who was going to be greatest in the kingdom? The way the church treated my mother may have a bearing on why my brothers and sisters aren't Christians today. There were eight of us and most of them don't know the Lord and don't care about the church.

My mother was a fantastic pianist. She also played the guitar. She could play in any key. But the church would do without a pianist before they would let my mother play the piano because she was divorced. To the church, my mother was just a harlot.

I don't know why she stuck it out. I would have quit and told them all to just play their game. But this was the

34

only Pentecostal church in town and that was what we believed. So Mother continued to go regardless of her heartache and hurt.

Evangelists would come to our town and mother would have them over for meals, take care of a lot of their expenses and do other things for them. Although our family didn't have a lot of money, my mother gave to God. She honored the Lord, and my dad allowed her to do this. The evangelists would want her to be a part of the revival and of what God was doing. The pastor or his wife, or someone from the church, would start stories about my Mom that were not true. Stories like she was chasing the evangelist, or some other scandalous tidbit that just wasn't true. My mother loved Jesus and my step-father, and wouldn't even think of doing such a thing. I remember some terrible fights at our house when the pastor and his wife would come and scream at my mother. I didn't know what it was all about. They called my mother all sorts of names because of her divorce and tell her that she was trying to take over, etc. I would see Mom crying and I'd run upstairs to hide from all of this. I don't know why I even went back to the church except I loved the Lord so much. The baptism of the Holy Spirit is the only thing that allowed me to keep my sanity. Praise the Lord, He became more precious to Mom and I through it all.

It was so hard to see my mother always kneeling at the pew. She would kneel there time and time again because she knew she wasn't welcome at the altar. The people could not forgive her for the divorce and remarriage (and she was the innocent party). Some people got a kick out of putting Mom down. Apparently it made them feel more secure. They didn't have any spirituality in themselves so they had to find a "bigger sinner" to pick apart.

Chapter 4

TEEN YEARS

When I was old enough to start having dates Mother was terribly, terribly strict. There was only one unsaved boy I ever dated, and only then because he was such a gentleman. I was the envy of all the girls at school when Ron would walk me into class. He'd kiss me on the forehead before he left me. He was a tall six-footer, and I was this tiny, little 73-pounder 4'11" girl. We dated for two years. He would never kiss me unless he asked my permission. I had to be in promptly every night at the time Mom said. She would set different times if it was something special. Her motto was: "It is just as easy Tammy to be one minute early as it is to be one minute late." She would ground me for a week if I was one minute late. So when I would go on dates, believe me, for sure I would jump out of that car and stand by the kitchen window so I could see the big clock above the stove. I knew I had to be on time, or else!

What bothered me about Ron was that he was not a Christian. He never drank, smoked, or did any of the things that Christians don't do. He had just never given his heart to the Lord. He came to church with me one time and I made him kneel at the altar and ask the Lord to come into his heart, but I knew that he had only done it for me. I knew because he still went to movies!! He couldn't be a Christian and still go to movies. That was a sure sign when I was a teenager.

When I was having all the trouble deciding what to do with Ron and my love for him, a new pastor, Rev. Johnson, came to our church. Things at the church started changing and fast. God moved by His Holy Spirit all over the place. The people even started treating my mother like a Christian. I loved that pastor so much for being good to my mother. He saw divorce in a different light, but the people fought him tooth and nail. Soon our church was having like 400 in Sunday school where it had been 65.

This new pastor saw a potential in my mother. His wife wasn't one of the jealous women. She was a preacher and understood what it meant to be used. For the first time in my life, Mother got to play the piano in church and the presence and the power of the Lord came down. For a period of three years Mother got a taste of what it was to be used of God.

Mother and I would sing together, and there wouldn't be a dry eye in the church. Mother sang with such a Holy Spirit anointing (I guess because of all the hard knocks and all the horrible things she had to go through), and everyone in the church was blessed.

Pastor Johnson had a son. It wasn't long until he asked me for a date. He fell head over heels in love with me (and so was Ron). I liked him because he was a little, dark, Italian-looking guy, and a Christian.

Here I was going steady with Ron, who was not a Christian, and now I had a chance to go with a Christian and no longer have that worry that I was dating a non-Christian. One rainy night I was out on a date with Ron. When he dropped me off at the house and went to kiss me good night I said, "Ron, this isn't going to work. You are not a Christian and I am. We are going to have to break up." He had had no hint that this was going to happen. All night long he stood in the rain at the side of our house, crying, yelling, "Tammy, Tammy!"

Mother and I both knew he was out there. I ran into Mom's bedroom and said, "Mother, what am I going to do? Ron's out there crying and pounding the side of the house." She knew how much I really loved Ron and how good he'd been to me.

"Tammy," she said, "don't you think you shouldn't jump so fast to another boy? You ought to be nice to Ron." I was foolish and figured another fish had come along and I was going to jump at the chance. I knew it wasn't fair, and it was a terrible thing I had done to Ron.

Soon the pastor's son, Ken and I were in "love" with each other. He was the kind of person who liked all the other girls too, but he liked me the best. By now I was out of high school and working at the Woolworth Store. We were together almost every night for over two years. Mother got to really liking him, but Ken had that little bit of flirt that I didn't like in a man, because I was a one-man person. This really bothered me.

One day Ken came to Woolworth's and said, "Tammy, I've bought you a little token of my esteem. I'll pick you up from work and then we can talk."

That night he was waiting for me after work. I got into his little "Henry J," and we went for a ride. He pulled the car to the side of the road so fast that we almost went into a ditch and nearly turned the car over. As the car came to a stop he said, "Tammy, I would like to have my graduation ring back."

My heart fell about 50 stories. "Why, Ken?" I cried.

"I just want it back," was his reply.

I gave it back to him. I was totally crushed.

He then handed me a little box and in it was an

engagement ring! I went into orbit! We drove to everyone's house we knew telling them the good news. Everybody was elated that Ken and Tammy were going to get married.

We decided we would wait about a year before we would marry. In the midst of the joy and happiness I was really unnerved because I had a calling on my life to serve the Lord. Whenever I would ask Ken what he wanted to be, he'd tell me it was really none of my business. This bothered me, although I loved him. We both wanted to go to Bible School, but for some unknown reason he did- n't want me to go. He said to me, "Tammy, I want to go to Bible School, but you've got to make me a promise that you won't come." Then and there I knew there was something wrong in our relationship.

I didn't know what to do. I'd go upstairs and pray by the hour asking God to give Ken a calling. I was deter- mined I was going to marry him regardless. Ken soon left for school. My heart was broken. It wasn't that I missed him that much—my heart was broken because he wouldn't let me do what I felt called by the Lord to do. It was then I knew I had to make a decision. If I went to Bible College there was going to be a breakup between us, and I had to figure out what was the most important thing in my life: Ken, or the Lord.

Two days before school was to start God spoke to my heart and said, "Hey, girl, this is it. You've got to make up your mind." Then I knew I had to go to Bible College. I had to follow God's calling on my life.

I called Aunt Gin to tell her I was going to quit Wool- worths (she had gotten me the job and I had worked under her since I was 15). I was so afraid she was going to tell me, "Tammy, you should have given me more notice that you were leaving." When she answered the phone all I could say was, "Aunt Gin," and then I burst out crying. In between sobs I said, "God has spoken to me and I've got to go to Bible College."

She just laughed and said, "Tammy, I'm so glad, honey. I'll help you any way I can." She had saved money for me during all the time I'd been working. Every week she'd taken a little out of my check and had put it in a savings account for me. She knew I would have spent it all on purses and jewelry. She added money to my savings and paid my tuition. I thought I was all set to go to North Central Bible College in Minneapolis, Minnesota, but then I thought, how will I get there?

Someone told me that our postman was going to Minneapolis to take his crippled son to the hospital. I called and asked if I could go with him. He said, "Yes, Tammy, I would just love to have you go with us."

I was still in turmoil. I didn't want to lose Ken. What was I going to do? That night I left my house to walk and think. I must have walked a mile down this dark, dirt road near our house. I would stop and cry and wrestle with the Lord. "God, You've got to show me what to do. You've got to show it to me." I was crying so loud one of the guys I had graduated with came out of his house to see what was wrong. He looked at me and said, "Tammy, is that you?"

"Yes." I told him the whole story. He put his arm around me and said, "Tammy, you've got to do what God is telling you to do." (And he wasn't a Christian!)

I knew that if somebody who wasn't even a Christian told me I had to do this, then I knew I had to do what was right!

Mom helped me get my clothes packed. The next day the postman was there to pick me up. I was on my way to Minneapolis.

I walked into the college building and Ken wasn't there. I was relieved. Soon, however, he came, walked up to me and I saw the aggravation in his eyes. I knew it wouldn't be long before our relationship was over. But I also knew that I had done what God told me to do!

Ken and I went out and talked, but it was a very strained relationship from then on. I was now aware that he didn't want me at school so he could discover other girls. Also, he didn't want me looking over the field of boys either.

Soon Ken started saying things like, "Tammy, if you would just walk a little different," "If you would just get those two teeth fixed, you'd be sharp," "If you weighed more you would be just right." I knew he wasn't happy. Something had happened. He needed his freedom and a time to look around. So one day I said, "Ken, it is all over," and gave him back his ring.

Once I gave Ken back his ring suddenly my security at North Central was gone. I didn't have anybody. Here I was with all these new people and really nobody that was close.

I got a job at the Three Sisters Clothing Store. While I was working I would go back to the dressing room and cry, then I'd go out and sell some more clothes. I'd go back to the dressing room and cry a while longer and then go sell more clothes. This went on for the first couple of weeks after I gave Ken's ring back. I was so lonely!

A boy by the name of Jim Bakker asked me out right after I gave Ken back his ring. I wouldn't go out with him because I thought perhaps Ken and I would get back together once his roving was over. Then one day somebody came up to me and said, "Tammy, do you know that Jim Bakker likes you?"

I had seen Jim around and thought he was the handsomest thing I had ever seen in my life, but I was so hurt that I couldn't get it all together.

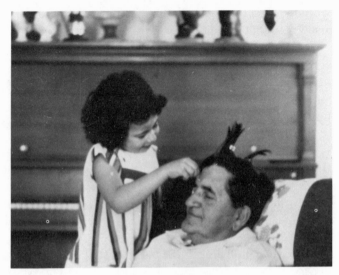

My Daddy, Fred Grover

Daddy holding Larry, Donny, Me, Mom holding Judy

Chapter 5

MARRIAGE

One night ten guys who were going bowling asked me to go with them. I was so dumb. To me I was just their little sister. They were soon bowling to see who got to get me a sandwich or who got to get me a coke. To me that was just fun and really neat.

When I got in from bowling that night, Jim Bakker, the hall monitor, told me it wasn't nice for me to go out with ten boys. He said it would ruin my reputation. I had so many brothers and sisters that everybody was a brother to me, and I had never thought of anything like that.

When Jim first saw me, for some reason I had the boldness to give him a little bell from one of my skates, even though we had never gone out. The night I walked in with all the boys he gave the bell back to me. Jim was the first person to tell me it wasn't right to go out with all the boys. It just broke my heart that he gave me back the little bell. I just knew that he would never speak to me again. I really didn't understand.

A few days later he asked me for a date. He weighed 130 pounds and I seventy-three. We looked great together. We went to church on our first date. It was a very cold winter day and the church was a mile and a half from the school. After church, on the way back to school, Jim very suddenly stopped walking and said, "Tammy, I can't see you any more."

I thought, "What now? This is weird. I can't believe this guy." I then said to him, "You can't see me any more. Why, might I ask?"

"Because I have fallen in love with you. My mother and dad want me to finish school. So Tammy I just can't see you again."

That threw me for a loop. I was stunned and puzzled, to say the least.

We continued walking. Again he stopped dead in his tracks and said like a General giving an order, "Tammy, kiss me!" He said it with such force that I never questioned if I should or shouldn't. I had never given a boy a kiss on a first date, but that wasn't going to stop me now. I reached over and kissed him, and WOW! I, too, was in love!

When we got back to school, he asked me to go out the next night. So I did. On the second date he asked me to go steady. He asked me to go out the third night. I did and he asked me to marry him. "Yes, Jim. Yes!" I said. I had no doubts. I would never have said that to any other guy I had ever dated. I felt it in the Spirit that it was of the Lord. When you love the Lord there is something inside you that bears witness, and God can speak to you and there's no great big thing. Jim also had a call of God on his heart and wanted to be a minister. We shared that calling together. We were just totally in love.

People tried to break us up. The Bible School went crazy. One boy called and said, "Well, if I would have known you were going to do that, I would have asked you out." From many I heard: "Tammy, please don't rush and do something crazy."

Sister Salto, the dean of women, called me to her

office and talked to me about Jim and our courtship. One of Jim's professors called him in and said to him, "I really feel this is the right girl for you and it's fine, but you need to finish your schooling. So you need to cool it a little bit."

Our grades started to drop because all we could think about was each other. There was no hope for us, we were so hopelessly in love. We didn't care what others thought. We knew what we wanted to do and that was it. Jim decided to take me to meet his mother and dad.

It was exciting because to me Jim's folks seemed very wealthy and prosperous. They really weren't, but they lived in a home like I'd never seen. Their house had two bathrooms, big velvet drapes, curtains, a baby grand piano, and a kitchen with a dishwasher. I mean their house had things I had never seen in my whole life. I was really awed by his parents. Jim took me to his church and it was really big.

I knew I was going to need a wedding gown so Jim's sister, Donna, told me to try on her wedding gown. We sneaked into this tiny room and I tried on the gown. I had no sooner put the gown on, when Jim's dad walked in. He just gave us a real hard look, turned around and slammed the door. We all just sighed. This was my first suspicion that there might be trouble.

Jim's mother and father were very upset when we mentioned marriage. They told Jim he could NOT get married and to drop the subject. Of course, our hearts were broken because we wanted their blessing.

We were only there for a couple of days during Bible School vacation. Jim's brother, Norman and his wife, Dorothy, were going to drive us back to school instead of taking the train back. We got in the car and I had the boxed wedding gown in my hand. We got just a few miles out of town and the car broke down, so we had to take the train back. Jim's dad came to pick up the car and take us to the train. His dad took the wedding gown out of the car and took it back home with him. It was his way of saying, "You are NOT getting married."

Jim and I wrote his folks again and asked their permission to get married. They wrote back: "No way are you going to get married."

Shortly after we returned from his folks, Jim came to me and asked, "Tammy, could I borrow $60 from you?"

"Sure." I didn't bother to ask why.

Little did I know—that was the down payment on my ring.

We were in church one night seated on the platform. Jim was head of a youth meeting at the church. Jim stood and said, "I want everybody to pray. Bob Silkey, would you lead in prayer?" Bob was his roommate.

As Bob led in prayer Jim stepped back and punched me. I opened my eyes and he slipped that diamond on my finger in front of all those people. He had alerted several in the audience and they were looking and laughing. So I went back to the Bible School engaged. The girls were envious of me and it was wonderful!

A month before we got married I called Mother and said, "Mom, I've found a boy here that I really, really love and I want to ask your permission to get married."

"Honey, you know about life and when you marry this young man you are the one who is going to have to live with him. I can't make the decision for you, but I give you my blessing, Tammy." She was so precious to me, and that really helped us.

Jim was very, very hurt by the fact that his folks said, "No," and by the fact that they had taken the wedding gown back. Jim prayed and God gave him a Scripture: "But from the beginning of the creation God made them male and female. For this cause shall a man leave his father and mother, and cleave to his wife" (Mark 10:6-7). Jim said, "We're going to get married."

All week we planned for our wedding and rented a little apartment from Jim's boss, Lena (a lady we loved so much). Lena was a real classy dame—the long cigarette, big hats, the furs, big diamonds, big car and Este Lauder perfumes poured all over her. I used to smell her and it was just fabulous. Every time you walked by you knew Lena had been there. Her apartment was in different shades of pink. When you walked in that apartment it looked like frosting on a cake. She lived there as a batchelorette and ran Rothchild's Restaurant, where Jim worked. She took Jim under her wing and liked him because he was so classy. Jim liked nothing but the very best.

Jim and I both love to decorate, and did we work on that apartment! It was just a dream. Jim and I really had to plan how we were going to leave the school. No one wanted us to leave so we knew we would have to sneak out. My roommate, Aloha, helped me get all of my things ready for the big move. Jim got all of his things packed and two days before our wedding we snuck out of Bible School. We moved in with Jim's sister, Donna, and her husband who was attending North Central also. They lived near the campus. This was a very hard decision for both of us. For one thing, I was a good girl and I wanted everything to be "prim and proper." But we also knew our Bible School wouldn't let you marry and stay in school. That was the problem. If we were going to get married we had to leave school. Since then they have changed those rules.

I was a bit apprehensive because I owed the school some money. I knew we'd just have to pay it out when we could. I also knew we were planning on going right into the ministry, which would have been years away if we had stayed at school.

We asked Pastor Olson if he would marry us. He loved

47

us both so much he said, "You bet, I'll marry you!" We decided we would get married in the prayer room of the Minneapolis Evangelistic Auditorium where Jim had received the baptism of the Holy Spirit.

We were going to get married in our favorite clothes. Jim in his black blazer with a little red emblem on it and a Scottish-plaid tie. My favorite was a red dress, trimmed with a little black velvet. We looked just like barbie dolls in those clothes. We were so little. When we told Lena what we were going to get married in she said, "No, no! Honey, you can't get married in red."

"Why, Lena?" I asked.

"You just can't, Tammy."

She picked out a light, almost white mint-green dress and said, "Honey, this is what you ought to get married in." She gave me her white kid gloves, a beaded bag and handkerchief to carry. She let me take a bath in her bathtub and even put Este Lauder bubble bath in it. I smelled heavenly.

We went to the church and were married by Pastor Olson. I got nervous and giggled through the whole ceremony. I laughed so hard tears were coming down my cheeks. I'm certain Pastor Olson was glad when the ceremony was over. The pastor was going to take pictures but the camera broke so we didn't get one picture of our wedding.

Our wedding night Jim had a big youth service. We got married just an hour or so before the service. "Tammy," he said, "you sit way in back and as soon as the prayer is over we'll take off to our apartment."

He opened the meeting and said, "Here is Bob Silkey to pray," then he ran off the platform and the people started roaring . . . as we tore out of the door.

We went to our apartment and on the table was Lena's gift to us: a beautiful wedding cake and a small glass of wine. There was a big bow around the glass and a note saying, "Tradition in our family is that the bride and groom drink out of the same cup on their wedding night." Jim and I had never tasted wine before. But just for Lena, we each took a sip and I almost gagged. I couldn't even stand the smell of it. It stayed in our refrigerator for weeks before I had the heart to throw it out. We got quite a whiff every time we opened the door.

We didn't have time for a honeymoon and we went right back to work.

Several weeks passed and I developed a very severe kidney infection and lost control of my bladder at work. I ran out of work just sobbing and saying, "Something is wrong with me. I've got to find a doctor." I went to the doctor and he confirmed that it was a bad kidney infection and told me to take the medication and stay in bed. I wet the bed every night. I couldn't get out of bed in time. In the middle of the night Jim and I would be changing sheets (how embarrassing). But with prayer, rest and medication I was soon well.

One day Jim found me behind the door sobbing. He couldn't figure out what in the world was the matter with me. He said, "Tammy, don't you love me anymore? Are you sorry that we got married?"

"Jim, it is not that. I'm lonely for my mother. I feel like we ought to go home so you can meet my family."

When Jim first met me he thought I was an only child because I was so petite and dressed so cute and had so many clothes. That always made me laugh. Jim was so understanding and kind. He took some time off from work (which we couldn't afford) and went to my home to see the family.

On this trip was the first time I had ever stayed in a motel. I felt like a naughty girl, and that I shouldn't be in a motel with a boy.

When we got to my house Jim could not believe his eyes. It was like the Beverly Hillbillies. Four brothers and three sisters running up to him, kissing and meeting him. At this time we still didn't have a bathroom in the house.

All of my people are just nice American family people. Everybody got acquainted, we ate one of Mom's terrific snacks and soon we went to bed.

The next day Jim got up and wanted to take a bath. "Honey," he asked, "where's the bathtub?"

I brought two tubs to the bedroom and went to fill them with water. Jim looked at me so strange and asked, "What are these?" pointing to the tubs.

"Jim, we don't have a bathtub. That's what these tubs are!"

He couldn't figure out quite how to take a bath in them. Never guessing that one was to bathe in and the other for rinsing. There Jim sat with his bottom in one and his feet in the other. I laughed until I cried. It was the funniest thing I had ever seen in my life: Jim Bakker in two tubs. When I told my family they got a big kick out of that. With the "outhouse" and all, it was almost more than Jim's dignity could take. But he loved my family and my family loved him.

I felt much better after I had been home to see the family. We went back to our little apartment and continued our honeymoon. And we have been on one ever since!

Jim was so in love all he wanted to do was stay home and play house.

The call of the ministry still was so heavy on my heart that I had to be about the Master's business. Jim had almost given up church totally and didn't want to go to church. It began to worry me. I thought, "Oh, no. What has happened? Jim is backsliding. Have I made a mistake?" I would cry over this and began to withdraw. I'd leave him at home alone and go on to church. One day Pastor Olson asked me if I would lead the song service. The power of God fell during the song service and God moved in a powerful way.

Over and over I told Jim I thought he ought to go to church. All he said was, "Tammy, I don't feel it is necessary."

I decided I was going to go over to the park across the street and end it all. Of course I didn't, but I went there and cried and cried and got it all out of my system and came back.

One day Sister Fern called Jim and said, "Jim Bakker, if you don't get back to church and do what God wants you to, your wife is going to be the minister. She's the one that God's going to be using, and you are going to be the one left sitting home on the shelf."

It scared Jim, so he started going back to church.

Those first few weeks in our marriage could have been disaster if God was not a prayer-answering God.

House where I grew up.

Chapter 6

GETTING STARTED IN EVANGELISM

As we started going to church together, the call of God became so real to both of us that we knew something had to be done. Jim and I prayed that the Lord would show us what to do. Soon things began to happen.

A missionary came to hold a meeting at our church, I'll call him John Doe. This changed our whole life. During the meeting John Doe told about his work along the Amazon and said that he was going to buy Errol Flynn's boat to use in his missionary work. He was a fantastic preacher and God really moved through him. That was the night that God got a hold of Jim and I, and we committed ourselves to be missionaries. The Lord showed us that we were going to work in the Amazon Region with John Doe. We were totally serious about this step, and in faith we gave all our household belongings away and decided to raise our missionary support. In order to raise missionary support we had to get a church.

Dr. Aubrey Sara came as an evangelist to our church and we fell in love with him, and he with us. During the church service I had sung and Jim had spoken and Dr. Sara saw through the Spirit that God was going to use us. Dr. Sara said, "Jim and Tammy, God wants to use you. I want you to come to my church and hold a revival meeting for me." We were elated. We couldn't believe it. But we knew God was leading us so we said, "We'll come!"

It was going to take us three days to get to North Carolina by bus and the next day the meetings would start. Pastor Olson found out about this and said, "No, sir, kids, no bus. I'm flying you there first-class on the church."

So we flew first-class on the airplane, like king's kids to our first revival meeting in North Carolina with ten pennies between us.

Aubrey asked us if we were hungry and if we wanted a hamburger. We got to the restaurant and ordered our hamburger and fries. The waitress asked us if we wanted it plain or "all the way." We laughed and asked, "What is all the way?"

"It's a hamburger that has slaw on it."

"What in the world is slaw?" Come to find out it was our cole slaw.

We were surprised at the red dirt.

We couldn't understand the southern drawl. We laughed and laughed. We heard people talk and we'd ask, "What did you say?"

Going to North Carolina was like going to a foreign country for us.

The first night of the revival Jim prayed and sought God all day long. We were going to set the world on fire that night. He was going to preach the greatest evangelistic message that had ever been preached, and I was going to sing the greatest songs that had ever been sung. It was going to be dynamite that night. We were so enthusiastic and excited. I sang and Jim preached. When Jim gave the altar call nothing happened. It was a failure. A total dud!

Jim gave up the ministry that night. He said, "I'm finished. It isn't for me. It is all over." He lay in the pastor's office on the rug, face on the carpet and sobbed and sobbed.

The next day he went back to the pastor's office knowing he had to face that revival that night. I didn't know what to do. I thought, "It's already over. This was it." I went to Aubrey Sara (thank God we got him for the first meeting) and said, "Something awful has happened. Jim's been in the office crying and crying. He says that he's finished with the ministry. I don't know what to do. I don't even know if he'll minister tonight."

Aubrey Sara went to him and talked to Jim like a son. "Jim, let me tell you something. I don't care if you feel like you preached the worst sermon in the whole world. You walk back to that door like a man. You stand there, smile at those people and shake their hand, and then leave the results to God." Then he told Jim he had preached a very good message for it being the second one in his life, and that we were going to make it.

We went back that night. Nothing happened.

The third night. Nothing happened.

The fourth night. Nothing happened.

We were totally torn apart. We were going to win the world for Jesus and it would take us forever this way. No souls, nothing!

The last night of revival, something wonderful happened! Ten people received the baptism of the Holy Spirit and all heaven broke loose and we had to stay another week. So we decided, "Praise God, we're going to stay in the ministry after all."

Aubrey Sara had gotten us another meeting in a church 50 miles away. We were so excited we could hardly stand it. We were raising money to be missionaries in the Amazon. (Can you imagine me in the Amazon! All day long trying to keep my false eyelashes from falling off and my nails from breaking. The only way I would have fit in is that I like jewelry just as much as the natives.)

54

We stayed with the pastor and his wife during that meeting. God just took over in that revival and people got saved. After we had been there a couple of days the pastor told us his mother was coming to visit so we would be moving in with some of the members of the church.

We were moved into the home of very wealthy people. They were having marital problems and through our loving each other so much (we were still on our honeymoon), they fell back in love again. They loved us so much, they gave us $10, and also a few personal items. The pastor found out about this and became jealous and told that we were taking money out of his congregation.

When we arrived at our next revival we learned about the rumor being spread by the pastor. We were shocked and terribly hurt! But we learned a very good lesson because of the $10. For one thing, one of the greatest tools that Satan has is jealousy and he doesn't care how or when he uses it. That is one of his devices that has followed us throughout our entire ministry.

From that day forward we have been careful of gifts and getting close to people in another man's congregation. God showed us through that $10 the proper pattern for evangelists.

God was really blessing our meetings and we were on Cloud Nine. Then it happened!

Pastor Olson called us and told us John Doe was a fake! Most of what he said was lies, and had spent the monies he collected on himself.

This helped us in a way. Jim and I had applied for our visas and had been turned down and we couldn't understand why. It didn't throw us a bit because we knew God had used that experience to get us into the ministry. That was the only way we would have started because before that we didn't feel capable.

We bought a little white Valiant from a used-car

dealer, and the meetings kept coming. Success in meetings makes other pastors want you. Soon we were booked for one year.

One of the most serious problems we had was never having the privacy we desired. In those days it seemed pastors always thought that the evangelist should be the one who should live like a gypsy. We had to take the brunt of everything on the evangelistic field. We never, never asked for money. We said, "Lord, we know that You are able and whatever the church gives us, You will make it enough." God never let us down!

We finally got to the point where we decided we needed to get a trailer. We were getting more and more nervous and everything was beginning to wear on us. Jim had developed such a bad ulcer that he could hardly face the public. It was that bad from staying with different people and having to live their lives all of the time. If you took a bath in their house they would get mad because we used too much hot water. For example:

I got a bad case of boils. I had to sit for hours playing the organ with these boils, to where I thought I couldn't stand it, and the only way to cause these boils to go away was to sit in hot water. I did this three times a day, barely putting two inches of water in the tub. The pastor of the church accused me of using too much hot water, knowing that I was sick as I was.

We prayed and asked God to give us the money to buy a trailer. We took this meeting in West Virginia, a tiny church up in the mountains. God began to bless and move. We started praying for the trailer in that meeting and people put hundred-dollar bills in the offering for us. We were embarrassed because we had been putting $20 and $30 in the bank. Now God was performing a miracle and giving us the most money we had ever had in our lives.

The next week we purchased the most beautiful

30-foot Holiday Rambler trailer. We were pulling it the very first day to go to another meeting when we noticed that the front part of the car had gotten quite high.

Jim said, "Honey, I don't think it's right for it to be like that. What do you suppose is wrong?" We couldn't figure out what it was so we kept going. We got on this four-lane highway going through this little town when suddenly our trailer came off the back of the car, passed us around the side, headed for a restaurant filled with people. Just before it hit the restaurant it crashed into a telephone pole and completely demolished the trailer, and we had only stayed in it one night.

I cried until I couldn't cry any more. "Jim," I said, "I cannot face living with the pastors and their wives anymore. What are we going to do?"

"Don't worry, honey. God's going to work it out for our good."

It just so happened that a photographer was passing by and took a picture of the trailer. The manufacturer had only spot-welded a seam instead of welding the entire seam. We thanked God we had proof. It was the trailer company's fault that it had come off the back of our car. The company had a lot of trailers to do and spot-welded ours and put it out before they had finished it.

The pastor where we were going came and got us and took us to his house. We had such dreams of being together in our own little place and now our dreams were all smashed. I didn't think I could possibly face that revival.

The next day we were in revival again. I got up to sing "How Big Is God?" This church was a hard, cold church. When I began to sing that song suddenly it just overwhelmed me of what had happened with our trailer. I put my head down on my accordian and began to cry. The church broke and everybody started crying, including Jim. Revival broke out in that church and continued for two weeks. Young people are in the ministry today because of that revival. They still come to us telling us that that was the revival where "I got right with God." God used that trailer to break the hearts of cold-hearted people in that church.

Three weeks later God gave us a new trailer with rounded edges, which we couldn't get before because this style wasn't out yet. We were given a much better and more expensive trailer for the same price as the other one because it had been the company's fault. The Bible says, "He doeth all things well." What a lesson of trust.

One night I was sitting at the piano playing for the altar call. People were being saved and a voice said to me, "You've sinned against the Holy Spirit."

I was so tired at the time that the voice got to me and I withdrew. It was racking me day in and day out: "You've sinned against the Holy Spirit. You say something against the Holy Ghost. Deny the Holy Ghost."

I was getting so jumpy and so nervous Jim came to me saying, "Tammy, there's something wrong with you, honey. What is the matter?"

I would cry out to God when there was no one around: "Oh, Jesus, I want to go to heaven more than anything in the world. Please, don't let me have sinned against the Holy Spirit, because I love You so much."

That voice would keep coming to me: "Say something against the Holy Spirit. You've sinned against the Holy Ghost."

I was sobbing at the altar in one of our services when Jim came to me saying, "Tammy, I know there's something the matter, honey. What's wrong?"

I told him!

"Tammy, it's the devil. He's just coming to you and you are tired. You are worn-out. It is just Satan trying to defeat you and to keep you upset. The very fact that you love Jesus so much and want to go to heaven is the fact that you haven't sinned against the Holy Spirit."

But the voice wouldn't leave me. Day in and day out, my mind was so tormented that I would rather have died than go through the torment of that year. Every day I had to plead the blood of Jesus over my mind. The Lord gave me some Scripture: ". . . whatsoever things are true, whatsoever things are honest, whatsoever things are just, whatsoever things are pure, whatsoever things are lovely, whatsoever things are of good report; if there be any virtue and if there be any praise, think on these things" (Phil. 4:8).

For one year I would look out the window and see one object, a tree, a flower, something I would look at and I would dwell on the beauty of that object to keep my mind together until God delivered me. And deliver me He did!

Today many people come to us and say, "I've sinned against the Holy Ghost. I'm going crazy. I love the Lord, but I've sinned against Him. I'll never be able to go to heaven."

I've been able to say, "Hey, I've been through the same thing. God's going to deliver you. 'Whatsoever things are pure, whatsoever things are good, whatsoever things are of good report, think on these things.' " I've been able to help others to receive that same deliverance.

There is nothing worse than mental torment. Now whenever the devil starts coming at me in the mind I get down before God and say, "Jesus, here I am. You've got to help me." And He does every time. I might go through a long time of it but He always brings me out. Without a fight there's no victory, no testimony, no freshness—unless things happen daily, weekly, and monthly to keep you in touch with God. There are very few things that people come to me with that I haven't been through and can say "I've been there and I know I have a God who is able to deliver you, able to see you through regardless."

Chapter 7

THE 700 CLUB

I just dearly love animals so Jim bought me a tiny little Chihuahua. I named him Chi Chi. That little dog travelled with us on the evangelistic field straight for two years. Chi Chi became my dearest little friend out in the field, as we couldn't have friends in the churches. God was very good to us and we had a very successful ministry. Many souls were won to the Kingdom.

One of our revivals took us to Portsmouth, Virginia, with Rev. Hugh Masson. Jim had a message that he preached to young and old people. But we felt we were leaving the children out. We had a burden on our hearts for children, but we didn't know how to reach them.

One day while shopping we saw on top of the Soakie Bubble Bath a cute little porky pig head and we both said, "That's it! We'll make a puppet out of this cute little head and start working puppets." We melted Porky's big ears down and made a little blond wig for it. I put little freckles on her, some eye lashes and made a cute little outfit. We called her Susie Moppet.

We found this old, funny-looking alligator which we called Allie the Alligator and made him a friend of Susie.

When we began to use these little puppets I didn't

know I had any voices at all, but soon discovered I had a little Susie Moppet voice and I had a big Allie Alligator voice. We built a puppet stage and began using the puppets in our meetings. Soon our meetings doubled and tripled. We were breaking Sunday school records all over the country. Kids were even dragging their parents to church on rainy, stormy nights. A man by the name of Bill Garthwaite came to one of our services. He worked for CBN and told Pat about us.

Pat Robertson soon asked us if we would come to his Christian television station in Portsmouth, Virginia and work with him.

We both said, "Oh, no. We couldn't give up our evangelistic services for television." We didn't feel right about that at all. And continued on the evangelistic field with our puppets.

Again Pat called us asking, "Won't you come and at least do one children's program for us?" He wrote us. He called us. Finally we said, "That wouldn't be such a bad idea. We could do one program for the children."

I'll never as long as I live forget the night before we went to do that show. I cried. I sobbed all night long. I was so frightened. I'd never been in front of a television camera in my life. "Jim," I said, "I can't do it. I can't do it. I can't do it."

Before we did the show we went to visit the television studio and Pat interviewed us on the air. Well, at least he interviewed Jim. He tried to interview me but I couldn't say one word. He gave me the microphone and I just went blank. I was numb. Jim did well, he was a natural.

Then we did our first kiddie show and it was a hit. I mean they probably got 10 calls . . . the most they had ever received. We left town and returned to the field. Several days later Pat called saying, "You've got to come and do a children's program. You must!"

Pat's station was really having financial problems and Pat needed something desperately. We were praying and God spoke to our hearts: "Yes, that's what you are supposed to do." We told Pat, "Okay, we'll come and be with you." We cancelled a year's revival meetings and pulled our trailer into Portsmouth to begin in Christian television.

Jim never thinks small. He thinks big and nothing is going to make him think small. He had said, "Pat, I'll come under one circumstance. You've got to let me do a Johnny Carson-type show some day for Christians." We would come home at night very tired after being in revival meetings and wanted to watch something on TV. All we could find was Johnny Carson.

Jim would say, "It is a shame that there is nothing like that on TV for Christians." We talked to Pat about this.

"Sure, Jim, I'll let you do that. That will be fine, just come."

We lived in our trailer for a few days but we soon knew it wasn't going to work. We were just too cramped. Our office at CBN was an old engineer's room that was full of nuts and bolts and junk. It was all greasy and dirty. Jim and I cleaned the room, painted it and took the old file cabinets (that no one wanted to touch) and sprayed the drawers. We sprayed each drawer a different color. We made that little office the cutest ever. That was the beginning of the "Jim and Tammy Show."

Meanwhile, we had to go apartment hunting. Jim didn't go to the cheapest part of town. With a $150-a-week salary you'd think he would have. Instead, he went to an apartment building with chandeliers and a doorman. "I want to see what you have," he said to the doorman.

"Jim, are you sure we should be here? This is really dumb. We're never going to be able to afford this," I said.

They had an efficiency apartment overlooking the

river on the seventh floor. It was gorgeous. It was $100 a month! We thought it would be about $140. We took it! Here we were living with the ritzy in town. We lived like kings. I'd call the store and order what I wanted and the grocery boy brought our order to the seventh floor. God wants His kids to have the best and we were living the way the rich lived on $150 a week.

The "Jim and Tammy Show" was now getting started. We had to build our own set. We decided the easiest thing to work with on a set would be a little house. We then went around the neighborhood and gathered a bunch of kids. They looked like little orphan kids. We wondered, how are we going to get them to come to the show?

We got a treasure chest and filled it with all kinds of little ten-and-fifteen-cent toys. Every child that came to the show got to take home a toy.

The "Jim and Tammy Show" got to be the biggest thing that had ever hit our city. Before we knew it, it just blossomed. We were on all over the country. Wherever the 700 Club was, so was the "Jim and Tammy Show." CBN was quite an experience for us. We offered friendship rings and certificates to the children stating that they belonged to the "Jim and Tammy Club." Later we had decoders, which we sent to the children. Susie would give numbers to the kids and they would decode them with their secret decoders at home. Jim and I sent all of these out ourselves, with the help of a couple extra women for the first five years of the show. Our hands literally ached from wrapping hundreds of rings very carefully so they wouldn't be broken when the children got them.

The "Jim and Tammy Show" began to help build CBN. Had it not been for that show I don't know what would have happend to CBN. God could have used someone else. He could have used Mary and Ted, or anybody, but God used Jim and Tammy.

63

I'll never forget one show we did. One of the precious little girls on the "Jim and Tammy Show" by the name of Susie, had died. She came to the show quite often. The way you came to the show was by writing for tickets. Little Susie had a rare disease and we did not know it. One day we got a call from her mother asking, "Jim, will you preach Susie's funeral? And, Tammy, will you sing? Susie loved your song, 'Love Lifted Me.' Every time she heard 'Love Lifted Me' she said, 'That's Tammy's song.' Tammy, will you sing 'Love Lifted Me' and 'Jesus Loves Me'?"

Susie was so dear to us. Our first reaction was to say no because we knew we would cry through the whole funeral. It would be uncontrollable. We had never ministered at a funeral before, and didn't even know what to expect. They wanted us to so badly we finally consented.

But first we needed to go to the funeral home. We walked up to the casket of that beautiful little dark-headed six-year-old and we realized she wasn't there. It really wasn't Susie. She was dressed in a lovely dress and had a little ring on her finger. She was so beautiful and had loved Jesus so much. But she was in heaven with Jesus. What remained was just a little body like a little doll's body lying there. We prayed with all our heart that God would help us somehow to get through that funeral the next day.

I sang my songs in victory at the funeral because I could just see little Susie in heaven as I sang. Jim preached a message of victory and joy. The next day the "Jim and Tammy Show" was dedicated to Susie. We showed her picture to the boys and girls and told them, "You are never too young to meet Jesus, and we never know when our time might come to meet Jesus. Even children meet Jesus." Over 1,000 people called and accepted Jesus Christ as their personal Saviour because of that show. We had people calling after the show went off the air way into the wee hours of the night. Boys and girls were calling, sobbing, wanting to go to heaven.

That show was re-run by mistake one day when we were home. We had told the office staff never to re-run that show unless there were people there to answer telephones who knew how to lead people to Jesus. We were home cleaning our garage when we got an emergency telephone call. "Come to the studio quickly, the 'Susie' show has been put on by mistake. Adults and children all over are calling in wanting to find the Lord as their personal Saviour."

We didn't push Jesus all the time. Susie Moppet would be naughty and Jim would reprimand her. We had fun, but then when it came right down to it, the viewers knew we were Christians and knew we loved Jesus. We might do six months of shows and then Jim would have one show with an altar call.

Sometimes I would get so tired doing the show that I thought I could not face another one because I ad-libbed everything. Many times because of our tiredness Jim and I would go on the show arguing about something. I would be so mad and disgusted with him and not even want to do the show. We still had to go on, smile and act happy for the children's sake. I'd get behind the curtain and Susie Moppet would be the one who would be terribly mad at Jim, and Alley would be the peacemaker. So it really worked for my personality; for Alley could talk Susie out of being mad, and by the time the show was over I wasn't mad at Jim anymore. I guess it was therapy for me.

During the time we were doing the "Jim and Tammy Show," I got a longing for a baby. I loved all the children so much, but there was a void in my life. Jim and I had now been married seven years. I felt our marriage needed a baby. Jim had had ulcers and then on top of that he had a nervous breakdown. CBN had put more on Jim than he could take. The doctor who had examined Jim told us we needed to get our minds on something besides CBN, and that we needed a third member in our family. Jim had never wanted children. We were too busy working for the Lord to have children.

I would beg and plead with him, "Please, Jim, let's have a baby. I want a baby."

Jim would look at me so sweetly and say, "No, Tammy, I don't think we ought to have a baby."

I wanted a baby so bad that I would pray that God would put a baby on our doorstep. I'd heard of people abandoning babies and believed that God would do that for me. My prayer would be: "God, you can have one of those babies put on my doorstep and Jim couldn't say no then." Every time we'd talk about babies we'd have an argument, and I would cry because I couldn't have a baby. I was getting more and more unsatisfied because I thought Jim was unfair. I was getting upset with him. I would pout and think, "All he cares about is his work, he doesn't care about my feelings."

Jim's nerves finally got so bad that he couldn't take a shower because the water felt like pins pricking him.

A strange feeling came over me one day when Jim came home from CBN. I noticed that small things were bothering him and he wanted to be alone. Then it happened! Jim had a nervous breakdown.

He lay in bed for a month in the back bedroom with his Bible in his hand, begging God not to let him lose his mind totally. I could hear him cry, "Please, God, don't let me lose my mind." He had worked so hard that he had come to the end of his rope and could not work any more.

The final blow came when we were told that Jim wasn't going to receive any salary while he was home sick. I sat stunned! I couldn't believe my ears. "Oh, God," I cried, "What is wrong with Your children? Why? Why? Jesus, Jim has been so faithful night and day for You at CBN helping raise the money and doing three shows a day. God, where are You? Please help us!"

Harvey Watson went to Management and said, "This is terrible. After Jim has practically given his life for CBN and has kept us from almost losing the station and you don't want to pay him while he is sick. You must pay Jim Bakker!" I praise God they had a change of heart and Jim got paid.

While Jim was sick I did the "Jim and Tammy Show" by myself for the entire month, and it was extra hard because I had become bitter. Very bitter. I hated all of the workers. I felt it was so wrong. We had worked so hard and had given CBN every minute we had and to have them do something like this to Jim. I felt I was coming unglued. CBN became the "other woman." I got to where I hated CBN. I hated the "Jim and Tammy Show." I wanted to take my puppet Susie and step on her head and crush her. I too had worked so hard, given every drop of blood. I had no one to talk to. I was alone all of the time. There were all these people around me, and yet, I was totally alone. I had nobody, not even Jim.

Jim could not go out of the house. He could not eat. He had to drink just cream for almost a month. He could hardly stand to have anyone come into our house because he couldn't stand to have them walk on the floor.

One day Jim needed a glass of milk. I filled the glass full, and as I was carrying it into his bedroom I dropped it on our hardwood floor. It spilled all over. I thought Jim would come unstrung. You can't imagine how much milk is in a glass of milk. My first thought was to just fall apart and cry. But God spoke to me saying, "Tammy, just be thankful that you have this glass of milk to take to Jim and that he is there to take it." As I began to clean up the mess God began to pour His strength into me, and I became strong as a rock.

I could not touch Jim or hardly be near him. Night and day I watched him in his bed reading his Bible and crying to God just to spare his mind. He thought he was going to lose his mind and end up in an institution. He thought he couldn't make it and nobody cared. There was only one person from CBN who came to see Jim. That was Hertha Allen. She worked with us on the show. If ever in his life Jim needed someone to show him love it was then, but there was no one.

I became so bitter because of what the staff was doing to Jim that I could hardly look anyone in the face.

As we were crying out to God He spoke to Jim about his eating habits. We had been eating hamburgers, french fries, all that junk food, because we never had time to fix a meal—always on the run, between one show or the other. He spoke to Jim about vitamins and proper nutrition.

Someone had sent Jim a book entitled *Hope and Health For Your Nerves.* He read the book and reread it and put it together with God's Word. Then he began to get a plan that worked for him from that day forward. God gave Jim back his mental and physical health. We began to eat good meals and to read God's Word together again. We hadn't had time to do even that! We were so busy working for God that we almost lost Him.

These events were Jim's time to set him solid for the rest of his life. He now knows how far he can go. Whenever that nervous problem starts coming back, or the ulcer starts burning, he knows when to pull back and to relax. God worked it out for our good. At times I didn't see any good in it at all, but thank God, He worked it out for our good. Today we take vitamins, trust God, and eat well.

We went through some terrible struggles trying to keep CBN a 100% Christian station. Part of the management kept wanting to put non-Christian programs on and Jim had promised the people that CBN was going to stay a

100% Christian station.

At one point, Jim had a 6 o'clock radio show in the morning and did the 700 Club at night. In between we did the "Jim and Tammy Show." He was getting so tired he couldn't stand it. I, too, got to the point where I couldn't take it anymore and said, "Hey, come on. We've got to start having some fun. We've got to start doing some other things."

Jim said, "I understand, honey, I'll take you out tonight."

The manager of the radio station called and said, "Jim, I want you to work the late radio shift tonight."

Jim said, "I'm sorry, I can't work the radio shift. I promised to take Tammy out. We've been working morning, noon and night and we've not seen each other. I promised to take her out tonight."

"Okay, Jim, if you don't work tonight you are fired."

We had been working almost night and day for months. Jim didn't show up and he was told he was fired!

Jim went to Pat the next day to get his final check. Pat said, "Listen, Jim. I don't want to lose you. I can't lose you, but yet you've got to be reprimanded for this. I'm going to levy on you a $100 fine. You either pay the fine or you are fired."

Jim said, "I can't. It is not right. I don't have money to pay the fine in the first place. In the second place it is wrong. You can consider me fired. I'll leave." Jim was Pat's main fund-raiser.

Before we left we went back to the studio to pick up all of our belongings. We loved Pat very much and went into his office to say good-bye. Pat sat us down and said, "Jim and Tammy, if you won't tell anyone here I will pay your fine, but please come back to work." At that, he reached into his pocket and handed Jim two fifty dollar bills. That really touched our hearts and we returned to work.

We were called the prima donnas of the studio by some of the people that worked at CBN. They always felt that we got treated special. We went out with Pat a lot and loved him with all of our hearts. However, many of the staff were jealous of our relationship. They were always trying to turn Pat against us. We were just like Pat's kids. In fact, he called us "kids."

I will never forget the time Jim and I moved into our very first little house. Friends of ours, the Taylor Brothers and builders of the house, let us buy it without any down payment. The house was in a subdivision in the woods, far from town. I was a bit frightened to stay there by myself at night. Jim was now doing the 700 Club, and would be there until 1 or 2 o'clock in the morning. Most of the time I was left in the house by myself, and it was slowly driving me buggy. I didn't drive a car at the time, so Jim had to send a car to pick me up for the "Jim and Tammy Show." I was by myself much of the time, because when Jim was home, most of the time, he was sleeping.

One day I went to Pat crying. I screamed and yelled at him saying, "Pat, I cannot take it any more. I am out at the house all by myself day and night. I hardly ever see Jim any more."

Pat patted me on the head like a little girl and said, "Tammy, I will see what I can do."

He didn't do anything, but thought I would be okay after I had done all my screaming and yelling.

As I was screaming and yelling at Pat, Henry Harrison walked in the door and I met him for the first time.

We sold the house in the country and bought a house on High Street. It was a beautiful, big, white, dutch-colonial house. It was my favorite house. Jim and I saw potential in that house. Our only hobby in life has been decorating. That kept us from going crazy during those times.

Henry Harrison came to CBN and needed a place to stay. Right away we felt Uncle Henry was our kind of people. He was a down-to-earth man who loved Jesus. We invited Uncle Henry to come and live with us until he could find a place to stay. He lived with us for five months. We enjoyed having him with us and had a great time. We shared the expenses and lived like kings.

We decided to put out bumper stickers advertising the "Jim and Tammy Show." Elections were taking place at this time. One man who was running for some office decided that Jim and Tammy would win the election as we had the most bumper stickers in the whole town.

Soon we could not go shopping without being deluged by mothers, dads and children. We'd be sitting in a restaurant and people would go by, look in, see us and then come in to meet us. It was an unbelievable success that was happening to the two of us.

We had put out a Jim and Tammy record, but CBN would not let us promote it on the show because of company policy. We offered to give all the proceeds to them but they would never let us use our Susie and Alley records so we just committed them to the Lord and said, "Lord, when Your time comes for the records then You will have to do it." If God opened the door that was fine, but if He didn't, that was fine too.

Praise God, today that record is bearing fruit. Here is a copy of a letter received:

"My husband, Gary, and I had talked to Jamie several times about salvation, but he wasn't interested. Then one day, all by himself, while listening to your album, he accepted the Lord as his personal Saviour. I was astounded about the way the Lord worked it out when Jamie came and told me what he had done. I just wanted you to know the good that your album ministry to children is doing. But that's not really what I'm writing about.

71

Last week we were eating supper when Jamie interrupted our conversation saying, "Mom, Jesus is talking in my ear."

We asked what Jesus was saying and he replied, "He's God. He's God!"

Jamie had been hearing voices in his ear for quite a while but didn't know what they were saying, so we bound the voice of Satan just in case. Anyway, we told him to tell us if Jesus said anything else. A few minutes later he said, "Can I tell you something?"

"Yes!"

"He said He's coming back pretty soon."

We were floored. Jamie is only four and doesn't really understand anything about the second coming. —S.C.

Hundreds have since been saved listening to Susie Moppet sing and talk about Jesus on the "Jim and Tammy Children's Record."

Daddy, Susie and Jamie

Chapter 8

TAMMY SUE

I wanted a child so very much, but Jim still wanted to wait. My two dogs Chi Chi (the dog I had bought when we were on the evangelistid field) and Fi Fi, a darling white poodle that someone had given me, helped me for a while and took care of that mother instinct. One day while eating supper, little Chi Chi who liked lima beans, ate some, and ran into another room. I had noticed that Chi Chi had been losing weight and couldn't understand why. When the dog didn't return I wondered. Jim had seen the dog fall over on the carpet and not get up. Jim went and checked Chi Chi and then gently said, "Tammy, Chi Chi is dead."

I thought my world had come to an end because that was the first time death had ever entered into me. I had never had anyone die that I loved so much before. I wanted to run out on the street and scream. As I started to run out of the door the Holy Spirit stopped me right in my tracks. I stood in the kitchen and couldn't move. I wasn't thinking about God, only about why was Chi Chi dead. The Holy Spirit began to speak through me in an unknown tongue. I couldn't stop. It helped to keep me from falling apart. God is so good. He is there even when we aren't aware of Him.

At that very moment a real estate man wanted to show our house to someone (they wanted to build a house like ours).

Jim handed Chi Chi to him and said, "Would you dispose of Chi Chi for us?"

Jim put his arms around me and I cried and cried. I said, "Jim, have them keep Chi Chi for a couple of days. Please, don't let them bury him right away because I know God can raise things from the dead. Please, don't let them bury Chi Chi."

Jim called the man and said, "Don't bury Chi Chi. Would you just put him outside in a box for a couple of days (it was in the middle of winter), because Tammy needs to settle something in herself."

I prayed and prayed and prayed. "Oh, Jesus, please raise Chi Chi from the dead." I expected Jim to bring Chi Chi home any minute. I knew God could do it, and Chi Chi would be all right again. I expected to open the door and there would be Chi Chi as usual. The fact was that Chi Chi was a naughty little dog. I loved him so much but several times I had wanted to give him away because he wet on our drapes, especially when he'd get mad at us. He'd chew on everything. We never knew what he would tear up next. But you see, God knew how to take care of Chi Chi for me. God knew that if He took him then that would be the end of the wetting all over the room. One time I had given Chi Chi away but I called the people and sobbing said, "I can't give him away. I love him so much." They returned him and I forgave him again. But I was still upset over the wetting and the destroying of things. God knew what was best for me and Chi Chi was finally buried.

With Chi Chi gone I began to desire a baby more than ever. I told Jim God would lay a baby on the doorstep of our house. So, wouldn't you know, one day we got a call from one of our partners on the "Jim and Tammy Show" telling us that her daughter had gotten in trouble and wanted us to adopt the baby.

"Praise God," I said, "that's it. That's it. Jim will surely go for this."

"Jim," I said, "honey, we're going to be able to adopt a baby. Isn't this wonderful?"

Jim said, "No! We can't do it, Tammy. These folks would watch our show and would see the child and watch it growing up and probably want it back. That would be a terrible thing to happen to us."

Oh, I disliked Jim for that. I spent one whole night sobbing. I couldn't figure it out because I knew Jim was way off in left field. However, one thing I've learned about Jim over the years. When he hears from God he's never wrong. At that time I didn't know that Jim was hearing from God. I thought he didn't want to be bothered with children. Jim called his brother about the baby and they adopted her. In the meantime we went to the hospital and picked up the baby. Here I was coming back to our home with that baby in my arms. The baby I wanted. Not being able to have that baby and having to hand her over to Jim's brother made me hate him too. I hated everybody because that was supposed to be my baby. But I got over it and Jim's brother took the baby and flew to their home.

Now I know why I wasn't supposed to have that baby. She was hyperactive when she was small. It was an unbelievable situation and God knew I couldn't have taken that and continued the "Jim and Tammy Show." So Jim was right again.

When Jim had his nervous breakdown the doctor told him that we needed a child. I kept praying and praying. Jim now said, "Well, Tammy, if you go to the doctor and have a physical and make sure that you are all right and that you can have children without any difficulty, we'll have a baby."

This was the first time I'd ever had a physical examination in my life! Can you believe that? I wanted that baby so bad that I was willing to go through anything. The doctor said I was fine. Fit as a fiddle. I'd been taking birth control pills for seven years and the doctor estimated it would take perhaps ten months for me to get pregnant.

We let Pat know that we were planning on having a baby and he was so happy because everyone in the ministry thought that we needed a baby. "That will settle them down. They won't be such peacocks once they have a child. They won't be the prima donnas any more," they said. People couldn't wait for us to have a baby.

Ten months later I was pregnant. This was one of the happiest times of my life.

By this time we had traded houses so often that we had built up our equity and we were able to buy a home in the better part of the city. A big, beautiful home on the lake. Nobody could believe that we could own a home like that on the little bit of money that the two of us made.

We didn't tell the children on the show I was pregnant. Soon I began to show and then we shared with them that I was pregnant. Then the gifts began to come. That baby had 100 pair of booties. We were giving things away just left and right. There was no way that one baby could use all the gifts! After Tammy Sue was born I never had to buy one thing until she was two years old. She was "their baby" because they had watched me on TV and shared my pregnancy.

The pregnancy was the greatest thing in the world to me. I never felt better in my life. Jim said, "Tammy, why didn't we try this before? If we'd only known it was going to be this good!"

I first met Linda Wilson while I was expecting Tammy Sue. Roger, her husband, came to work for CBN during that time. Linda and I became super close friends. If it hadn't been for Linda, I don't know what I would have done, because she'd been the only one I'd been able to talk to, share with and to whom I could pour out my heart. Linda would shop with me, cook with me, was at our house, or I was at hers. For the first time in my life I had a true friend.

It was Sunday morning. I began to go into labor. I got dressed and full of excitement went to the hospital. Little did I know the agonizing year that would follow.

I was in labor for two days. This was my first hospital experience. The fact that they would make me be naked in front of doctors and nurses and not close doors really terrified me. I was so modest, prim and proper. I could not stand the fact that everybody was looking at me. It meant nothing to them, but to me it was one of the most traumatic experiences of my life.

I called my mother but she couldn't come as she had children at home. So Grandma Fairchild came to be with me. For a while the doctor thought they were going to lose the baby and me. Jim called the 700 Club and said, "We've got to pray, or we are going to lose both Tammy and the baby." When they began to pray Tammy Sue was born.

Tammy Sue to us was the cutest baby in the whole world. She looked like a little Japanese doll, slanted eyes and dark black hair. She looked just like Jim. The doctor said to Jim, "Your baby has her father's features and her mother's fixtures."

Jim asked, "Well, what do I have?" He was puzzled.

"You have a baby girl!"

Jim was elated. When he came to my room he found me talking out of my head. I didn't know where I was, or what I was doing. It really frightened him. The second day when he came I was crying and couldn't quit. "Honey," he said, "we have a baby girl. Aren't you happy that we have a baby girl?"

"A baby girl?" I questioned.

"Yes!"

I still didn't realize that I had had the baby. I had to have nurses with me throughout the first night because I saw spiders crawling all over the drapes and I tried to jump out of bed to kill them. I had mice under my bed and was trying to kill them too. The nurses said they had never seen drugs react on anyone like that. It was like I was having a bad drug trip. The third day I finally realized I had a baby. I got to feeling super good then and on the fifth day I was allowed to dress the baby. The nurses were saying how exciting it was that I was such a good mother.

The sixth day I wrapped my precious baby and took her home and a week later went back to work. My grandmother was there to take care of the baby during the day and at night we'd have her in our room. We were just enthralled having that precious little bundle in the bassinet next to our bed. We'd wake her up in the night so that we could love her, and look at her often to make sure she was breathing and was alive. Jim and I were so happy.

I got back into all my clothes again and felt like a million dollars.

After the first two weeks Tammy Sue was waking up at night, like babies do, and was crying. I wasn't getting enough sleep. We didn't mind not getting enough sleep because it was so wonderful having her there. But I was beginning to get nervous. I would sit on the couch and shake from the effect of drugs and lack of sleep. I broke out in little red bumps. It looked like measles. I was being given too much medication. I didn't know what to do or how to handle it, but I was feeling good. I thought: the medication is coming out, so I'll just forget it.

One night just before bedtime Grandma found me in the kitchen crying. She asked, "Tammy, what is the matter?"

"Grandma, I can't face it. I'm so tired. I can't face night coming any more. Unless I can get some sleep, I just am not going to be able to go on."

At that she took the baby into her bedroom, and we practically had to get tickets to see Tammy Sue.

I went ahead and did the "Jim and Tammy Show" and was doing fine. We took our precious little baby and showed her on the air.

Life was great until Grandma Fairchild tiptoed into our bedroom one morning with her coat on and said, "Tammy, I'm leaving you. I'm going back home."

I was terrified.

"Honey," she continued, "Tammy Sue is beginning to look up and smile at me like I'm Mama. I'm not Mama. You are her Mama. It is time that you and Jim took the baby back in your room."

For the first time I had the baby by myself. Life began to get complicated. I had to do my housework, plan the "Jim and Tammy Show," and take the baby and have her on the set. She was a wonderful baby and didn't hardly cry ever at night. She became so perfect it was almost unbelievable.

But something began to happen inside of me. Suddenly I couldn't pray any more. I couldn't cry any more. I couldn't laugh any more, and I couldn't even let Jim touch me. Every time he'd go to touch me I felt I was breaking out in a cold sweat all over my body. I thought I was crazy, and didn't know what to do about it. I was turning into a zombie. Poor Jim. He thought I didn't love him any more. After three or four weeks of this he said, "Tammy, if you don't love me, don't let the baby stand in the way of a divorce."

I was shocked and couldn't figure out why he'd even think of an awful thing like a divorce.

"Tammy, I don't know what's happening to you. I

can't stand to see you like this. You don't laugh, you don't cry. You are just nothing. What is the matter?"

"Nothing is the matter," I said. Yet I couldn't sing on the 700 Club. I went through a routine on the "Jim and Tammy Show" and got out of there as fast as I could. Finally, I went to Jim and said, "There is something wrong. Bad wrong. I'll go back to the doctor."

I explained to the doctor what was happening to me. "What went wrong when I had Tammy Sue? Why did it take two days? Why did you give me all the medication?"

The doctor just shrugged his shoulders and said, "Well, you have to pay a price for anything that's good." That was all he would tell me. The nurses later told me that they had given me an almost fatal overdose of medication. Since the doctor couldn't or wouldn't give me any answers I went home. I thought our marrige was going to fall apart. I didn't know what was going to happen. I got to where I didn't even know if I could pay any attention to my baby. Jim didn't understand what was happening. He almost refused to understand. It was making him madder and madder at me. He simply couldn't cope with a wife that was going crazy. I had always been the strong one, the happy-go-lucky one, the light one—that was the Tammy Jim knew. He thought I just didn't love him and was being stubborn. He thought I was afraid that I would get pregnant again after having such a hard time with Tammy Sue.

"Jim, I'm going to try one last thing before we do anything else. I'm going to call a psychologist," I said.

"Okay, honey," Jim replied. We were really desperate!

While thumbing through the "yellow" pages I realized I'd never thought in terms of a psychologist, and didn't know who to look for. I found a name, dialed about three numbers, and God spoke to me, "Tammy, let Me be your psychologist."

For the first time in months I knelt down by the couch and began to cry out to God. A God I didn't even know was any longer there. I had not even felt saved all these months. I had tried to communicate with God but I couldn't reach Him. It had been as if He wasn't even there. I couldn't shed a tear (my way to God had always been through tears). As I cried, "Jesus, You've got to help me. I need Your help so bad to get out of this thing." Seemingly nothing happened. I still was a zombie, but I knew I'd heard the voice of the Lord again. I knew there was hope.

Someone called telling us that there was to be a Holy Ghost revival at one of the big centers and wanted Jim and I to take part in it. Well, all I needed was a revival. I could have cared less about a revival. They wanted me to sing. I hadn't sung in months. I said, "No, I can't do it." But the Holy Spirit did it again and said, "Go do it." So I told them, "Okay, I'll do it." It was several weeks away. I had all that time to make up my mind to do it and then to say, "No, I can't."

But the inevitable always comes. Jim was working so Roger and Linda took me to that meeting. I was a nervous wreck. I thought I was going to die before I got there. It must have been the devil trying to keep me back. I kept saying, "Roger, slow down. Roger, you're going too fast. Roger, please, Roger!"

"Tammy, I will never take you anywhere again. You are making me a nervous wreck too." We were good enough friends where he could say that to me. We finally got to the meeting.

I walked nervously to the platform not knowing if my legs would even carry me. The organist began to play and as I started to sing, "The King Is Coming, The King Is Coming, Praise God He's Coming Again," the Holy Spirit fell on me! About 1,000 people stood to their feet and

81

began to praise the Lord. A lady in the audience who loved the Lord and had been around CBN for a long, long time said when God released me that she saw sparklers like at the Fourth of July just bursting out of the top of my head and falling all over me. The Holy Spirit freed me that night. As I ministered I felt the Holy Spirit as I hadn't in months. I didn't want to sit down, but I knew I had to because the minister was supposed to preach. I sat down.

The minister tried to preach but couldn't. Finally, he said, "I can't preach, this is Tammy's night. God has given the message to Tammy."

I got up and ministered in word and song. Scores of people came to the altar and found Jesus as their Saviour that night. I was never the same again. I have had a victory and joy unspeakable and full of glory that I never had before and it has never left me. But I went through one year of such unbelievable torment that I thought I was going to die.

Mom and Dad

Chapter 9

LEAVING CBN

CBN was in a time of severe financial difficulty. This was Jim's and my first telethon. The electricity was going to be turned off and CBN was about to lose everything. Nobody wanted to admit that we had problems. Jim said, "How do you expect to raise money for a Christian television station when nobody knows that you have a need?" He was told, "Don't you tell about our needs!" The staff seemed to be so proud in those beginning days.

Many of the men at CBN would build Pat up so much until he thought, "Well, that's the guy I've got to go with." It was the people around him who said, "Pat, don't tell the people we are in trouble."

Jim started doing the telethon and nothing happened. He came home the first night and began to pray, "God, what is the solution? What is the solution?" God told him, "Jim, be honest with the people!"

Jim went back the next day and said, "People, we're going to lose it all. They're turning out our lights. The station is going to go back, unless somebody gives."

Many of the men backstage were saying, "Pat, stop him!"

Jim was just sobbing and the phones started ringing

off the hooks. Pat said, "That's the Holy Spirit. Let Jim continue. I feel this is God's way of saving us."

People started coming to the studio, bringing their money with them. The rest is history. Jim had simply let the people know we had a need. It was through that telethon that the 700 Club program started. Jim said to Pat, "Let's stay on the air and do the show I wanted to do—the Johnny Carson-type show."

Jim began to do the 700 Club, and did it for years by himself. The staff began to realize that Jim was getting too popular with the people. They suggested Pat take over one or two nights of the show. The last years Pat did it every other night. Jim was very popular with the people, so we could see why the men thought Pat had better step in and we understood. It helped us when he took a couple of nights. It gave us some nights together.

There was constant conflict at CBN, and many seemed jealous. There was always the fighting to see who could get the closest to Pat. There was especially a jealousy of Jim and I, because we were so close to Pat. Jim was Pat's number one right-hand man and raised most of CBN's finances. As a result, Jim and I had to suffer because of the jealousy. Every time someone new came to CBN we had to go through this. Things were said against us to Pat so that Pat would think less of us, and, therefore, bring them closer to him. But the plan generally backfired.

Pat was the kind of person I liked and yet disliked. One minute I would love him more than anything in the world, and the next minute I would dislike him for letting people manipulate him.

Once Pat went all over the country trying to obtain $100,000,000 that a widow was supposedly going to give CBN. Jim felt it was wrong, but was afraid to go to Pat and tell him. Finally, God spoke to him and said, "Jim, I want you to go to Pat, regardless of the cost, and tell him this is not of Me."

Jim went to Pat and told him what he thought God had said.

Pat said with a broken sound in his voice, "Jim, have I become so untouchable that you and Tammy couldn't come to me? I'm sorry. I wish you had come sooner because the inevitable has happened and it is all down the drain again. CBN has spent thousands of dollars trying to get a few million. It was all a big hoax."

My overall feeling about Pat is one of deep love and deep respect. I've sewed on his buttons, mended tears in his clothes. I've loved him with a real deep love of the Lord. But at times when he would do certain things because of other people I built up a terrible, terrible resentment in my heart against him. However, I have always known he is a real man of God.

It was a constant up and down until we thought we were going to go crazy. Pat would bring people in with new programs and new shows, and the shows weren't Christian. They had nothing to do with God. We had promised the people that it would be a 100% Christian station. Jim raised the money on the premise that it was going to be just that. To have it otherwise would be wasting the money he had gotten on the air by begging, pleading and crying.

For several years God began to speak to us about leaving CBN. He put a restlessness in our heart. When that restlessness started we knew it might be two or three years, or it might be ten years, but we knew it was going to come, that God would move us, and that our job would be finished there. For some time the Lord spoke to us through the Word in Ezekiel 12:1-6 (Living Bible), that we were to get our house in order for leaving CBN.

It shocked us that God would speak harshly. But every Bible we had would fall open to this passage. So we knew it was God. We were so unhappy in our hearts.

The "Jim and Tammy Show" was going great and was the height of everything a Christian children's show could be. Then a new man came into CBN and was placed in charge of the television, and the "Jim and Tammy Show." He told us we had the worst show on the face of the earth. That totally demoralized us. We were in tears.

"Jim," I said, "I'm not ging back to the show. There's no way I can do it."

A few days later this same person came to us saying, "Your show is getting better now. You are starting to improve it." We were still doing the same thing we had all along.

One example of how God was using this man to help move us out of CBN came as we were taping the shows. It was a one-hour show, Monday through Friday. We would tape five shows on Saturdays. We scheduled the children to come in shifts—an hour and a half apart. There would be 100 to 150 kids at each session. By the end of the day I was totally wrung out emotionally. Then this man would come in and demoralize us so badly we could hardly get through the show. Once he went to get a haircut and made the children wait for an hour and a half. We ended up with 300 children, and their parents, waiting to come on the show and we had no place to put them. He did things like this to show us he was boss.

Jim and I went through three years of torture at CBN until it was almost impossible for us to work. We were praying daily that God would give us strength somehow to make it through that day.

To make matters worse, there was also a lady at CBN that was very unkind to me. She did not like me. I felt she hated me with a passion. Every time she would come around me, she'd say cutting things to me until I got to the point where I disliked her so much that it was starting to come between me and God. I thought: *Here we are giving everything in our whole world for this ministry and she's so mean to me.* For example, there was a meeting of all the lady counselors and I walked into the meeting. This lady turned to me saying, "Tammy, you have not been invited, and you are not welcome."

It was always things like this that crushed my heart. I would pray, "God, bless this woman. Lord help her to change. Lord, help me to love her. You bless her and make her a different person." But inside I was just saying, "I despise her. I wish God would do something mean to her." I kept telling Jim I couldn't stand her.

"Tammy," said Jim, "don't let her stand between you and God, honey. Your bitterness will only put you in bondage to her."

As I was praying, I knew I had to get this right with God and with her. This went on for months. One day God spoke to me, "Tammy, why don't you tell it to Me like it really is, and then I can help you. Quit lying to Me."

"Okay, Lord," I sobbed. "You know I dislike her. You know I can't stand her and You know I wish You'd do something real awful to her. She is so mean to her husband. I have seen her kick him because he'd been out with us and not left her the car. You know there's no way I can like her. But I know that You can help me, and through You I can love her." I spilled it all out.

It didn't happen overnight. Nothing with me has ever happened overnight. It has been gradual. But the Lord let me see that it wasn't really the woman that was doing this. The only tool that Satan has to work through is people. It wasn't the lady being so mean and hateful, it was Satan getting at me through her.

The Lord said, "Tammy, you don't have to love what she does. But you must love her because she is My child and I love her just as much as I love you."

I began to get my perspective right and said, "Lord, I ask You to forgive me, and I'm going to love her through You!"

The next times I saw her she was still mean and hateful to me. I still felt a tear well up in my eyes. But suddenly it wasn't bothering me as much. I wasn't being affected by her response. I couldn't figure it out. Soon we were smack-dab together—sitting next to each other. I looked at her and said, "I've had some bad feelings in my heart against you because you've hurt my feelings. I want to ask you to forgive me. I want to tell you that I really do love you."

When I told her "I love you," that was the releasing word for me with the Lord. When I confessed that I loved her I can honestly say that from that day forward I have loved her, and didn't have any hurts in my heart over her anymore. I couldn't have loved her in myself, that took Jesus! Later I understood why she was the way she was, because I've gone through the same thing. A mother raising children with her husband not being able to help her presented a problem. She was fighting for her own identity. The secret of a love for people is to separate the person and sin. Jesus always loves the sinner and hates the sin. There is an old Indian saying, "Don't judge another man until you have walked a mile in his moccasins." What a difference that makes in understanding our fellow man.

On the eighth of October I was standing in the kitchen washing dishes when Jim came in, looked at me and said, "Tammy, God has spoken to me that today is the day I've got to resign from CBN."

My heart almost burst inside me. Here we were giving up the biggest thing that had ever happened to us. We were at the top of the heap. The very height of what anybody could do with Christian television. We were known around the country for the "Jim and Tammy Show." Yet I was so thankful that the day had finally come when God released us.

That day Jim went to work, looked up Pat and said, "Pat, God has spoken to me. The time has come for me to leave you and CBN. I am not leaving to divide the ministry, but we are leaving to multiply."

At that time we had absolutely nothing in mind as to what we were going to do. As far as we were concerned, we would never be in Christian television again. We knew God had spoken. We were stepping out in blind faith that God would provide.

A few days before this God was speaking super heavy to Jim about resigning. Jim cried out to God and said, "God, You know I've got a $50,000 home here to pay for. I have bills. What am I going to do all of a sudden without any income?"

The Lord spoke to him saying, "Jim, you resign first and then I'll take care of the rest."

We have found in every instance in God's will in our lives we've had to take the first step by faith. We had to step out like in a big, black hole, not knowing where we were going, or what we would do. Not even having a plan, but one hundred percent relying that we had heard from the Lord and that He would see us through.

I would rather step out in blind faith with God, than walk by sight alone.

Pat said, "Jim, the board has just voted to give you a $25-a-week raise." That was an awful lot to us, because at that time Jim and I were making about $200 a week between the two of us working all the time. That would have meant security for us again.

It looked good to Jim. He said, "No, Pat, God said 'Today.' So it has to be today."

Our hearts were heavy because we loved Pat. We have always loved him and always will, because he was the man who taught us. He cared enough about two young people and respected our ability enough to take us in and teach us. He also allowed us to do what God had spoken to us to do, and we will always be grateful to Pat. We left that day in tears.

That same night we watched the 700 Club with a new host, and saw the rerun of the "Jim and Tammy Show." We sobbed until we almost couldn't stand it, knowing even though God had spoken to us, it was all over—that part of our lives. It was totally over!

Some sad things happened after that. We weren't gone a day when some of the staff, who had been jealous of us, completely destroyed the set we used on the "Jim and Tammy Show" . . . a set that had cost thousands of dollars to build . . . as some of the others watched in unbelief and tears. The Coca-Cola Company had made a Susie Moppet head that was three or four feet in diameter. We would take her everywhere we went with the program. We'd play the records behind her and she would move and sing for all the children. The Susie Moppet head was axed and torn to pieces. Eight years of video tapes of the "Jim and Tammy Show" that had brought thousands of boys and girls to Jesus (that could have been rerun for years) were erased. Satan really had a field day making certain that we would never return to CBN. This broke our hearts. We were aware of the jealousy, but did not know there was that much dislike in their hearts for us. We had only done what we felt God would have us do there. I am thankful and grateful God allowed us to be a part of a great ministry like Christian Broadcast Network.

Chapter 10

CALIFORNIA TELEVISION

After we resigned from CBN we put our house up for sale. The morning after we resigned, Jim was shaving in the bathroom and called to me, "Tammy, hurry and get the house cleaned up. God is sending buyers to our house today."

I was so excited I ran through the house and got it spick and span. That very afternoon a knock came on the door. Some people from New York had gotten lost in our neighborhood looking for a house for sale. When they saw our house with the FOR SALE sign on it, they bought it that day and gave us a down payment. They were counterparts of Jim and me. They loved everything we loved. They needed a house of our type because they had a crippled boy who was in a wheelchair. They could roll the wheelchair around in ease and the boy could have a nice view of the lake. They also bought almost all of our furniture. They paid the exact price we were asking and did not argue about one penny. We had a garage sale and sold the few things that we had left over.

It was sad when Tammy Sue saw us sell all of her toys. To this day she will ask, "Mama, you're not going to sell it are you? You're not going to give it away are you?"

Our past living made such an impression on her. We even gave away my parrot, that I'd had for so many years.

After the sale God spoke to Jim to take a vacation. We bought a beautiful trailer with the money from the sale of our house. We made Tammy Sue's bed in the bathtub. When we left town we didn't have any idea where to go, or what we were going to do.

We headed toward Florida where it was warm and sunny. We had a great time just resting and relaxing. Shortly some ministers found out that we had left CBN and offered us meetings. We also had offers from television stations wanting us to work at their station. That wasn't what God told us to do, so until we had rested we turned down all of the offers.

Then this one television station called asking if we would please come and raise money for their budget. We began to go from TV station to TV station to raise their budgets for them. We did telethon after telethon, helping Christian television stations get back on their feet.

We were in Arizona for a while and thought being that close to California we would go to visit Channel 30, the station that had run the "Jim and Tammy Show." It was there that we met Paul and Jan Crouch. We immediately fell in love with them. Jan and I were so much alike it was remarkable.

Jim and Paul talked about starting a TV station of their own. There was a channel available Paul thought they could get. Paul said to Jim, "I'll tell you what, I'll work at Channel 30 for a while longer, and meanwhile we'll check into the possibility of getting this other station together." At that Jim and I moved our trailer down to the beach. The four of us would get together in the trailer and earnestly pray as to what direction we should go.

Soon God spoke to our hearts that we should move ahead. Jim and Paul got it all together and we rented a building. Paul had some money saved up and, of course, we had some money from the sale of our home. We used the corporation that Jim and I had called "Trinity Broadcasting."

After we left CBN, Stu and his wife, Carol, came to our home and said, "Jim and Tammy, you need something to protect your ministry, even if you are going back on the evangelistic field. You need to form a corporation."

Jim and I hardly knew what a non-profit corporation was. Stu said, "All you need is four people to start a non-profit corporation. If you ever do anything in the future where you may need one, you'll have it." Stu set it up with Jim as the president, Stu as the vice-president, Carol the treasurer, and I the secretary.

Although we call the corporation "Trinity Broadcasting," we had nothing in mind at this point. Not even an idea as to where we were going or what we were going to do.

Using our corporation, we got the television station set up and miracles of God began to happen. We knew God was confirming what He had allowed us to do. People gave us fine electric typewriters and desks. We turned a huge computer building into a beautiful television studio. The tile on the floor was quite bumpy and broken. Jan and I cleared that entire studio of tile. There was this black, hard, tar-like stuff left on the floor. The day we needed him, God sent a man that knew how to get rid of it. In one day he had cleaned the floor. God sent air-conditioning men and electricians just when we needed them. It was a miracle of Almighty God. The people would just walk in the door, not even knowing why they were coming.

The only way we were able to advertise what we were doing was through the church, where Paul and Jan were attending. Their pastor was also very interested in TV. Paul and Jan set it up so that the four of us could talk about the station at their church on Sunday mornings.

For some reason the pastor seemed to dislike us immediately. Even though we decided that was the church we were going to attend.

We soon sold our trailer. Paul and Jan had a gorgeous home (the most beautifully decorated home I'd ever seen in my life!). They had a guest house with a garage on one end and an apartment on the other. Jim and I moved into their apartment. We then became terribly close to Paul and Jan. Paul said I was so much like Jan that it scared him at times. I'm the type of person that uses my dishrag for everything—wiping up the spot on the floor, washing the dishes, wiping dirty little mouths, whatever. And Jan did exactly the same. We both love lots of jewelry. We had the same taste in decorating. We both love to bargain hunt for anything in the world. We especially had fun at a flea market that we called the "Chino Dump." We would get our eye lashes and wigs there and all the things that girls need.

Jan and I were alike even temperamentally. But we got along fantastically, and we loved each other. Everywhere we went people asked if we were sisters.

When we formed the "Trinity" corporation we never dreamed it would ever come in handy. But now Carol and Stu were on our board with Jan, Paul, Jim and I. We prayed and prayed, asking God what we ought to call our new program. We finally came up with the PTL Club, which we felt was a code so that when Christians looked at the program they would automatically know what it meant.

Then Stu decided that they should have their own work in Charlotte, so they resigned from our board. The traveling and all was just too much. Now our board of directors was just Jan, Paul, Jim and I.

Paul said, "Jim, I am perfectly satisfied to be the business manager. It was your corporation and all. You should be the president. I will run the business and you run the ministry."

It was a beautiful, wonderful relationship, and we thought nothing in the world could ever come between us.

God began to bless and the Holy Spirit was outpoured and thousands of dollars were pouring into the station. We saw God work miracles. Soon the pastor from Paul's church began to come around talking to Paul about Jim. He would say, "Jim is far too emotional for California. He shouldn't be praying for the sick, or talking about the baptism of the Holy Spirit on the air." That was the first wedge formed to come between us.

We began to learn things about California that we didn't like. Some things really shocked us. They had a different way of living and had different standards than we. We invited Paul's pastor to be with us on TV. To our surprise he said things on TV that would let people know that he wasn't for Jim's way of running the PTL show. Slowly it began to drive the wedge deeper, as Paul and Jan loved their pastor and listened to what he said.

The station needed cameras. We knew we couldn't afford them and were simply trusting the Lord to supply them. Paul and Jim called Ralph Wilkerson of Melodyland Christian Center and asked if we could use their cameras to get started.

"Sure," said Ralph, "they are just sitting in the church, not being used. We'll be happy to loan them to you for as long as you need them."

We thought it was wonderful that God supplied and we got to use the cameras.

One day we received a call from Ralph. He said, "If you are going to keep using my cameras, I think I should be on the board of directors of PTL."

Paul came to Jim saying, "Jim, man, we've got a gold mine in Melodyland. If you'll put Ralph on the board, we'll be able to get out from under this financial burden."

Jim replied, "Paul, we don't need Melodyland or any other church as our source. God is able to undertake. Look what He's already done! Do you think He's not capable of continuing the good work which He has begun?"

Paul then began to want to add men to the board. Men that he knew had money or influence. None of these men knew Jim.

Jim would give in, one at a time, even though he knew he was cutting his own neck. Finally, he just didn't say "No" any more.

We had been sending PTL tapes to Charlotte, North Carolina, because Jim was still president of PTL. God was moving in Charlotte through the tapes from California. People wanted Jim to come to Charlotte, and were praying that God would move us there. We had no idea of their prayers. We wanted to stay in California. That's where the action was. That is where we felt we could do our thing, where God could use us.

We kept getting different members on the board, and the board began putting more pressures on Jim, threatening him and causing him to have to do things that he knew were not right before God.

One night we were doing a telethon and the money was pouring in. People were bringing money in by the hundreds of thousands of dollars and God was moving when Paul's pastor got on the air and in front of that entire television audience denounced Jim. "I do not, nor does the board agree with the things that are going on. We don't like the way PTL is being conducted and we are going to do our best to change it and make it the way it ought to be."

Jim walked off the set, went into a side room and began to weep. Never had I seen a man weep that hard. He turned to me and said, "Go get Tammy Sue. I'm afraid something is going to happen to her too." He thought I was going to leave him. He was like a man in the throes of death. He was like a man who was having his last breath taken from him. He took one look at me and said, "Honey, it's all over. They've got us."

I looked at Jim, a totally beaten man and said, "Jim, at least they haven't crucified you yet. They haven't taken your life. You get up from here and do what God has spoken to your heart to do."

It was an unbelievable thing in California. Even though at times we had no money, we were the happiest we've ever been because we knew we were in God's will. People would come to us and just give us things. Like Ella Eix and her son, Freddie. They took a liking to us and those people supplied all of our food. They didn't supply little stuff, they supplied us with big steaks and gave us so much that our freezer was filled to overflowing. They gave us money, beautiful dishes and outfitted my kitchen. They took care of Tammy Sue. I mean they really loved us and proved it! How often I have thanked God for those two wonderful people.

Jim went back on the air and continued PTL.

One day Ralph came to the office and said, "Jim and Paul, I really feel that if you are going to continue to use our equipment that I should be on the board of directors."

Paul immediately agreed that Ralph should be on the board.

When we first arrived in California Ralph was one of the first men Jim and I wanted to meet. We had heard so much about him and Melodyland that we could hardly wait. Now we were learning that he had feet of clay just like Jim and I, or any of God's other children.

Ralph was right. We had no money to buy any other cameras.

Jim knew that was the end.

Ralph said, "Jim, I would never hurt you. I will only help your ministry."

Jim replied, "Okay, Ralph."

In good faith he took Ralph on the board of directors.

The station began once again to come into a money crisis. Paul said, "Ralph is on our board now and I think we ought to turn PTL over to Melodyland. Jim, you will still be the president and we will still be able to run the station. I will remain the vice president and the only change will be that Melodyland will underwrite this thing one hundred percent."

"Paul, I promised the people that this was going to be their station. They have given of themselves, their money and everything because they thought it was going to be their station. I have nothing whatsoever against Melodyland or Ralph. But we can't give it to a church. There is no way in the world I can give this station to a church. If you are going to vote to give the station to Melodyland then I am going to have to leave," replied Jim.

The directors had their meeting and Jim cast the only "no" vote. They then voted Jim off of the board and another chapter closed in our lives. Paul was made president and Melodyland got the station. Jim left the meeting and went to his office and packed his belongings.

When Jim and I left most of the staff went with us. We got together that night and sent a letter to all the people on the mailing list. We felt the people had a right to at least know what had happened. Yet, we knew in our hearts that God never takes anything away from us that He doesn't give us something better.

Again, there was nothing in view.

That night as we were all in Jim's office praying, God gave me the second vision I've ever had. As far as I could see there were angels with robes. They had helmets on their heads and swords in their hands. I saw the back of Jesus! He was standing tall and straight with a helmet on His head and a sword in His hand. He wore the most beautiful white gown. Over the gown He had a beautiful blue sash that came down and covered His shoulders and fell to the floor. He spoke to me in an audible voice. "Even as you stand here, My angels and I are going forth to do battle for you." That was all He said, and the vision disappeared.

That vision gave us the courage to live through the next three months.

That night we left PTL. There were 25 of us. All had their apartments, had to eat and had to pay their bills. Once again, we were stepping into that deep, dark hole and didn't know what life was going to bring forth for us.

We all went to our house and had a prayer meeting. We began to storm heaven to find what God wanted us to do. Those prayer meetings were the only thing that kept us sane. We were together praying for a month when God spoke to us to start a new corporation.

We formed a corporation called Dove Broadcasting. We had more fun that month than almost any time we ever had in our lives. There was a light-heartedness I cannot explain.

Hertha Backland owned the Swedish Villa Restaurant. Any time any of us from Channel 30 wanted to go out and eat we could go free to her big, beautiful smorgasbord. That was special because none of us had hardly any money. She fed us when we were hungry. She was God's manna from heaven.

People heard of our prayer meeting and began to attend.

Hundreds of letters were coming in. Ruth Stenson, Jim's secretary, let us use her house as our office. Five days a week we conducted business from her house answering letters of those who wrote and said they were praying for us. Every day enough money came in the mail to pay everyone the salary that they had been receiving at PTL. Not one of us missed a pay check.

No one suffered one moment except, of course, mentally. Wondering what God was going to do with us.

We drew plans for a television station, in faith believing that God was going to do what He promised.

One day Stu called Jim, "I want you to come to Charlotte for a telethon. The people have been asking for you." Jim and I went to Charlotte for the telethon.

We left our house and drove to Charlotte. The power of God came down, miracles of all kinds took place, and hundreds of people were saved.

"Jim," said Stu, "you've got to move to Charlotte and take over hosting the PTL Club live from here!"

God spoke to Jim and told him to do just that. Jim was stunned, but we knew we had to come to Charlotte. There was no other way for that was what God had spoken. They rented a small apartment for us and Jim left me in Charlotte. I never again saw my home, birds, and puppies, Biscuit and white Fi Fi. It was as if California had disappeared for me.

Jim flew back to California, and told the people that there was work for us to do and to come to Charlotte. Jim sold our home and the rest got rid of their apartments. In a week we were all together in Charlotte.

Jim began to host the PTL Club.

Chapter 11

PTL CLUB

Here we go again with "showers of blessings," and God began to move. We were put on a very good salary. Our house in California had sold for a good amount of money so we bought a home in Charlotte. Two days after we bought our house, in comes our furniture and we got everything all set up and guess what happened? Our house sale in California fell through. So now we had a house in California and one in Charlotte on which to make payments. What in the world were we going to do?

"God, here we are again," we prayed. It was one of the first times we didn't panic.

Jim said, "Lord, if You want me to have that house in California You can help me make the payments just as You can help me make the payments on this one." We committed it to God and forgot it. It was as if it hadn't even happened. The first temptation would be to worry yourself sick. But we were able, through the power of the Lord, to forget that situation.

Two days later our house in California sold for more money than it had sold for the first time. What a lesson in teaching us to truly trusting God and letting it all lay on Him.

PTL took off in a fantastic way. We were happy. God was blessing. God was moving. It was the most exciting thing in the world. While things were going so fabulous at PTL we began to hear rumblings of things happening in California. Melodyland had now given PTL back to Paul. Our lawyer had told us that's the way it would have worked had we wanted to stay and fight the case. It would have been impossible to put Jim out as president, but Jim isn't a fighter. He simply said, "I will not take my brother to court." So rather than take anyone to court, Jim just left saying, "You all want it. You can have it. God bless you," and he really meant it.

I don't know how Jim ever did that.

"Honey," he had said to me, "they can take houses, lands, buildings and channels away from me, but there's one thing they can't take from me, that's the ministry that God has given me in my heart. Wherever we go we'll have that."

I used to tell Jim, "Jim, why don't you fight for what you know is rightfully yours? Why don't you stand up and fight for your rights?"

"No, Tammy, I have a God that will fight my battles for me," was his reply.

Jan and I were the ones who did the fighting. I told her where to get off and she told me where to get off. To this day I regret that we ever said those terrible words to each other. If I've asked God once, I've asked Him 100 times to please forgive me for ever saying those things to Jan. I learned a real lesson through this. You can say you're sorry a thousand times, but you can never take back angry words, and you never really forget them.

Jim and Paul never had bad words. Jim just left without saying anything. Paul and Jim are still very close today.

I still love Jan so much, and I thank God for the work

that God has allowed them to do in California. We've prayed for the blessings of the Lord upon them. They have asked us to come and be on their station and they have come and been on our station. So God restored our relationship, and today it is very precious. God has given Paul and Jan a beautiful ministry. Souls are being saved. It is still going on, and God, too, has given Jim and Tammy a beautiful ministry and souls are being saved. So we came full circle to what Jim said to Pat at CBN: *"We are not leaving CBN to divide the work of God, but to multiply it."*

Things were going along just fine at PTL when suddenly we began to have suspicions.

Jim was raising money, raising money and raising money. Remarkable amounts of money were coming in to PTL. Yet creditors were calling, "Why don't we get paid?"

Here Jim was raising money to pay these people and for some reason they weren't being paid.

Jim went to Stu. "Stu, I know there is something wrong."

Stu bristled immediately and said, "There's nothing wrong. Carol and I have everything under control."

Stu was running another channel and Carol was running our little station.

Stu left his channel and came to our station and began to run it.

One cold morning Carol was going out the back door of her home to get a paper when she slipped on some ice and shattered her ankle. We rushed her to the hospital and found she was going to have to be in the hospital for two or three weeks.

While Carol was gone Jim took this opportunity to look in the files to find out why the bills weren't being paid. He discovered poor management and went to the board of directors.

They said to Jim, "We don't believe that. We can't believe that. It is unbelievable."

"Come and see for yourselves," replied Jim.

They, too, discovered that the bills weren't being paid.

As a result Carol and Stu were asked to leave PTL, and Jim took over all phases of the operation.

Jim and Jim Moss, who was a member of the board of directors, called all of the creditors and promised that within six weeks all bills would be paid.

Jim got on the air and explained what he could of what happened without hurting Carol and Stu. And that we were terribly behind in finances. Unless God undertook, it was all over. There would be no more PTL.

The people rallied and gave PTL enough money to pay all creditors in six weeks! PTL started on a new foot and a new walk with Jesus, with signs and miracles following.

I used to be a very selfish person. Being from a family of eight children we never had a lot and I valued anything that I got. I just wanted to keep everything for Tammy. I never knew the joy of giving.

Jim began to preach on the joy of giving and what God would do if we gave to Him. Then God spoke to us, "You are preaching that message and now I want you to live it."

We didn't know He was going to ask us to **live the giving part of our preaching.**

We began to give to God and God gave back to us. What a lesson we learned when we began to give to God. I'll never forget the first $25 God asked us to give. We were sitting in church and there was a special need. Jim whispered to me and said, "Honey, God has spoken to me to put in $25." I gasped as it was all the money we had, but I looked at him and nodded a silent yes. That was our grocery money. But somehow I felt good inside. We were giving it to Jesus. The service was hardly over before someone came up to us and whispered, "Can I take you two to dinner today?" Our eyes lit up as we seldom got to go to a restaurant for dinner. We said, "Yes," and were on our way. After we had eaten and were about to say thank-you and good-bye, he handed us a $20 bill. And that night in church we were handed two more $20 bills. Sixty dollars the Lord had returned to us. After that, giving became easier. We always remembered what God had done with our $25, and even though many times we questioned the Lord after that, we always ended up obeying.

I remember the time an evangelist and his family of eight children came through PTL. God spoke to us to give them all of our money we had saved up for a vacation. I can remember saying, "Oh, please Lord," but found myself writing out the check.

The family accepted the check with tears streaming down their faces. They had a great need that we weren't aware of. We decided we'd just stay home this vacation, but God had better plans. Jim was to speak at a prayer meeting that night at A.T. and Nadine Lawings. When the service was over, A.T. stood to his feet and said he felt led to take a special offering for us. We received about $400 that night. The next day I went to the mail box and opened a letter to find another $400 that someone had owed us for two years on some furniture they bought from us when we sold the house in Virginia. We just couldn't believe it! Before the time came for us to leave on vacation we had given to us about four times what we'd given to the family of eight. A great lesson we learned. No matter how hard you try, you cannot outgive God.

Now I give whether God gives back or not because I love to give so much. One day I gave away three closets full of clothes. I don't buy expensive clothes. I've never had to because I'm small. Recently, I bought five skirts for $4 a piece. I buy most of my clothes at stores like Sears and Penneys. The most I've ever paid for a street dress in my life was $28, and that was last year. I've paid more of course, for formal wear.

God spoke to me, "Tammy, there are more clothes than you need in that closet. You need to give them to somebody in the ministry who needs them."

I discovered that one of our painters' wives didn't have much clothing. I gave her the first two closets full. She was so happy and pleased. I saved out a few of the special clothes that I really liked and said, "God, I'll give the things away that I don't wear much, but these things that I wear quite a bit I think I had better save them in case anything should ever happen."

God again spoke to me, "Clean out another closet, Tammy."

So I cleaned out another closet full of clothes. I'd saved them for years because I don't gain weight so I can wear clothes a long time.

I gave that closet full away and not two days later a lady sent me five items of clothes that totaled over $1,000. It included the most gorgeous lavender suit with the skirt, the pants and a top that has a mink collar on it. She sent me gowns like I had never had and told me that on every show I would have a new outfit to wear. I asked her, "Why?"

"Because I love you and God has spoken to me to do it." What a wonderful God we have.

I gave a diamond ring away. I just don't go giving diamond rings away because I don't get them that often. God spoke to me to give that ring away. It was a hard thing for me to do. Two weeks later a girl came to me and placed a ring on my finger. The one I'd given away had three diamonds in it. This one has 20 diamonds on it and is worth three times as much as the one I gave away. I didn't ask God for that. I had given as unto the Lord. I didn't even want to get any of those things back, but we serve a God who is faithful and who is abundantly able to give above what we could even ask or think.

If anyone had ever told me that one day this little girl from International Falls would be on nationwide television I'd have said, "Oh, come on."

One day I got a telephone call. I picked up the phone and the voice said, "Hi, Tammy. This is Pat Boone."

"Yes, sure and I'm Marilyn Monroe!"

It really was Pat Boone calling Tammy Bakker, person-to-person, saying, "Tammy, you and Jim come and go to Israel with us. Tammy, please don't be afraid to fly. We all love you and will be right there to help you through the trip." Pat Boone had called Tammy Bakker!

I'll never forget the time I took Carol Lawrence shopping, or the time I helped Dale Evans Rogers into a new dress, or the time I had Norma Zimmer on my show and we cooked together. Or the time I did my puppets for Art Linkletter, or meeting Jeanie C. Riley, or the time we went to the Grand Ole Opry and Hank Snow treated us like the stars—even took us home with him and we sat and ate homemade cookies with his precious wife, Min.

Me, in an airplane talking to Larry Flynt about Jesus.

Now, can God do the impossible? Just tell me.

Here are my folks sitting back in International Falls watching Tammy in front of the world having a chance to tell people that, "Jesus loves you. He really does!"

I'm not a singer. I don't consider myself to be a singer. I would have never dreamed that I would ever be able to make a record. But God called me to sing for Him. And so I did. Although many times after singing in front of a large congregation, I would sit down and weep bitter tears saying I would never sing again.

I'll never forget the day I met a man who has helped me more than anyone in this world when it comes to singing. He had long hair, a beard, wore bright red boots, a jumpsuit, a huge hat and sunglasses. This was a contrast to my image of a Christian, yet this man deeply loved the Lord. God was beginning to teach both Jim and me another lesson.

Gary S. Paxton hadn't been saved very long when he walked into PTL and introduced himself to us. What a story he told. How God had saved him from drugs, alcohol, and women—Gary S. Paxton had done it all. He had been a millionaire three times and lost everything. His songs, "Allie Oop," "Monster Mash," "Honeymoon Feeling," had been on top of the rock charts. Then he met Jesus. Now he wanted to do something great for the Lord.

Our spirits bore witness to this man and before I knew it, I was on my way to Nashville, Tennessee, to make my first real LP recording. It would include some of Gary's songs he had written for Jesus, "The World Didn't Give It To Me," "Layed Back in His Love," "Jesus Keeps Takin' Me Higher," and "He Was There All The Time." I was frightened to death, but Gary's gentle spirit soon relaxed me. He told me I could sing, he put songs in my correct key, he wrote songs especially for me to sing that would fit my voice and he prayed with me. Gary S. Paxton gave me a confidence I'd never had before.

Jim and I now consider Gary and his beautiful wife, Karen some of our best friends. Only God could cement together in love two such completely opposite couples. Gary opened our eyes to another world and expanded our spiritual vision. And we in turn have made him aware of the world we were familiar with. And to think that God loves people in both our worlds just as much. What a wonderful lesson. It's not the long hair, the beards, the outward appearances. It's the heart that counts with God.

God put me in the place where I didn't think it was possible for me to fulfill, and if I would have had any inkling I was going to do this I probably would have fainted dead away and never come awake again.

God takes us as we are. So praise God.

Four Generations: Mom, Me, Grandma, and Jamie

Chapter 12

JAMIE CHARLES

Tammy Sue was about five years old. One day I said to Jim, "Can you believe that Susie is going to start school next year? We are not going to have a baby around the house any more. What in the world are we going to do?" (I'm a mom, you know. I just have a mother's heart I guess, and couldn't stand to be without a baby to love.) "Please, please, please, honey, can't we have another baby?"

Jim has always said to me, "You are going to plan the number of children we have in our family. That will not be my decision. That will be your decision so you can never turn at me and say that you are miserable now with all these kids because I made you have them."

If I thought I had to beg for Tammy Sue, I had to beg double for Jamie. Finally, he said, "Well, okay, honey. But remember that it is your decision."

When I realized I was pregnant, I was really excited. Linda went with me to the doctor when he confirmed the pregnancy. I went into orbit. I hadn't told Jim, or that I was even going to the doctor. Jim was on TV and I walked in on the middle of a PTL Club program and whispered in his ear, "We're going to have a baby."

Jim almost fell out of the PTL Club chair.

Dan White started playing "Rock-a-bye Baby" on the piano, and the whole world knew we were going to have a baby.

I had had such a wonderful pregnancy with Tammy Sue I thought this one also would be perfect. Anytime any girl would moan and groan and be sick through pregnancy I didn't have any sympathy for her at all. I thought that was foolishness and all in her head.

A few weeks after I got pregnant I began to go through the worst sickness I had ever experienced. I could not eat. I could not even take one bite of food. If I did, for two or three hours I'd just be in bed doubled in a ball praying that God wouldn't let me die. My back felt like knives were stuck in it, and my chest felt like I was going to smother to death. I went to the doctor and said, "I don't know what's the matter with me. I'm just terribly, terribly sick." He couldn't do anything for me. All through my pregnancy I was sick. On top of this, Jim was busy building Heritage Village and was gone all of the time and couldn't even be there to sympathize with me, or even help me. The house we lived in was fairly close to the PTL Club, but Heritage Village was 30 miles away. If Jim came home, it was a 45-minute drive. He'd be gone until 2 or 3 o'clock in the morning sometimes. Here I would be at home sick and thinking he didn't give a hoot. I began to build up real resentment.

On top of all of that, one of my girl friends had a dream. She dreamed that there was this funeral and Jim was standing up on a hillside holding a little baby boy. Tammy Sue was standing by his side and there were lines and lines of people coming to see me at my funeral. She dreamed I would die in childbirth. I was about two months pregnant when she told me that dream.

I did not dare tell anyone this dream because I

thought they'd think I was crazy to even think about it. It was on my mind all of the time. Maybe I was going to die having this baby. Sick as I was, the Lord knows, I sure felt like dying. Almost every day was torture.

I felt Jim should care as much about me as he did about that building project. I just had to fight for any time I got with Jim. One night he didn't come home until about 3 o'clock in the morning. I had called and called PTL, but at that time there was seldom anyone there to answer the telephone. So, no matter how long I'd call, I'd not get an answer. All I could think of was that Jim's car had run off the road and he was somewhere hurt or dead. Sometimes if someone would answer the telephone they would say, "Jim left an hour ago." He left all right, but was standing in the parking lot for hours at a time talking and all excited about the building, like any man would be.

I thought Jim didn't care, that I was a second spot to him. I just could take no more. This was three or four weeks before Jamie was born.

When Jim came in that night at 3 a.m., I took one look at him, walked into the guest bedroom and shut the door. I would not talk to him. He tried to tell me why he had been late and I wasn't interested. I thought, "That doesn't make any difference to me. You don't care. That's it!"

I couldn't sleep, and the thought that he was upstairs sleeping made me madder than ever. At least he ought to be miserable too. Come to find out, he was miserable too. Terribly miserable.

The next morning I wouldn't speak to him. He went to work. That was something that had never happened in our marriage before, not ever. Just before the PTL Club was to come on, I got a telephone call from Jim Moss. "Tammy, Jim's here and he's crying. He's almost out of his mind worried about you. He loves you so much. He didn't realize what he was doing to you by not being with you when you needed him. Unless you two make things right he's not going to be able to go on the air."

I felt so terrible and ashamed. Jim came to the phone and I told him I was sorry. He said he was sorry and that he would pay more attention to me.

"Jim, I won't demand as much attention from now on, I promise you," I said. So we had a love affair over the telephone. I couldn't wait until he got home that night to hug and kiss him and say, "It's going to be all right."

The next day I went to sing on the PTL Club. I was so sick I could hardly stand up to sing, but I'd made up my mind that I was going to do it. Always in my heart, my ministry comes before anything else. So, instead of standing, I sat down to sing, and still felt very sick. I finally said to the TV audience, "People, I'm sick and I can't get ahold of God for healing. I've got to have somebody help me. Will you please pray for me that the Lord will touch me and make these last couple of weeks of my pregnancy bearable? I don't know what to do or where to turn." Then I sang my song.

I was told prayer meetings rose up all over the United States. Praise the Lord, God touched me! I could now eat without getting terribly sick. I had only gained two pounds during the pregnancy up to that time, because I was so sick.

Jim began to pray that the baby would come before Christmas so I could be at home for Christmas Eve with Tammy Sue. I knew God was able to do that. It is so wonderful how God cares about the little things. It doesn't have to be a big thing with God. He's concerned about all the little tiny things in our life and that's why I love Him so much. Our prayer was that God would bring the baby either before Christmas, or wait until after.

Just a few days before Christmas I began getting little

cramps at the bottom of my tummy and I realized the time had come that I was going to have my baby. At 5 a.m. I awakened Jim. "Honey, I think we'd better go to the hospital." I had had bad high blood pressure for the last two weeks. When we called the doctor he said, "Due to your high blood pressure you'd better come in right away."

We called Roger and Linda and they met us at the hospital. They took Tammy Sue. Tears came to my eyes as Tammy Sue left me, not knowing if I would ever see her again. Then the nurse wheeled me into the labor room.

Jim stayed with me until it was about time to do the program.

The doctor talked about a Cesarean section because I was in labor so long the previous time. He thought it might be another two-day ordeal for me if he waited. He talked to Jim about this and Jim said, "Yes, I think we ought to go ahead with it."

Jim asked me, "Honey, do you want me to stay here with you, seeing that you are going to have to have a Cesarean? Would you like me to stay here and have someone else do the PTL Club?"

I'd never had anything like this before, but the strength of God came into me and I said, "No, Jim, you go and do your work for Jesus and Jesus and I will have this baby."

My blood pressure kept going up and up so they prepared me and took me into the operating room. I'd never been in an operating room in my life. Here I was, not a stitch of clothing on, stark naked, with my legs prepared up in the air the way they do . . . the whole works . . . with all these people meeting me. The doctor introduced me to the man who was putting the solution in my arm to put me to sleep. The doctor wanted me to meet him because he watched PTL. The room was also filled with nurses who watched PTL, waiting to see what we would have. In the

114

midst of all this I had a peace and wasn't terrified like I was when I had Tammy Sue. I thought I would be terrified, and that maybe this was the last day I'd be on earth (because of that stupid dream), but I experienced what the Bible talks about when it says, "a peace that passeth all understanding."

"Tammy, are you ready?" the doctor asked.

When I woke up I was on the table and the doctor was telling me, "Mrs. Bakker, you have a beautiful baby boy!"

I just started crying and saying, "Thank you, Jesus! Thank you, Jesus!"

The doctor called PTL. "Tammy's had her baby and it's a boy!" he told them. So the crew wrote on this big cue card: **IT'S A BOY** and flashed it in front of the camera and the place went wild. People were cheering, jumping and shouting: "They got their boy!" So everyone knew before Jim, who had left PTL and was on the way to the hospital after the show.

When Jim got to the hospital the doctor told him he had a baby boy. The doctor said Jim laughed with a holy laughter. He laughed and laughed and laughed. The presence of the Lord just came over him.

Then Jim came to find out how I was doing. For a change, I was doing fine.

And what day did I come home? Christmas Eve!

I spent Christmas Eve at home. In faith believing, I had bought a tiny red stocking and hung it on the fireplace next to Tammy Sue's.

Our whole little family celebrated with little Jamie Charles—Uncle Henry and Aunt Susan Harrison (how Jim and I love those two!) were with us also.

When we first got home Tammy Sue walked up to Jamie Charles, looked at him, then to me and asked, "Mommy, is Jamie a Christian? Does he love Jesus?" And

115

before I could answer her she put her little hand on Jamie and said, "Dear Jesus, come into Jamie's heart." She then looked at me and said, "It's all right now. We all love Jesus." What a precious Christmas!

Jim's mother and father came and stayed two months and took care of us when I wasn't able to do anything. I couldn't even walk, much less take care of a family and keep a house clean. Jim's mom washed clothes, brought food to my room and took care of our children. Jim's mother and dad did everything for us.

I'd always felt Jim's mom and dad didn't think I was really part of their family. I had felt left out because I had married Jim against their wishes. I didn't know how to act around them much of the time. Many times I'd wished I'd gotten married into a family that really loved me and would accept me as their daughter. I would cry over this sometimes.

Jim's dad was a rather gruff man and would tease me. I didn't take teasing well because I was so tender-hearted and would end up crying most of the time.

During this time they showed that they really loved me, and that I was truly their daughter. Did I ever fall in love with them! I have felt part of the family ever since.

Chapter 13

MY MAN

Many people ask me, "What is Jim really like? What kind of a man is he? What kind of a husband is he? Is he a regular person, or is he the kind of man who sits around and prays all the time?"

Jim and I both are very fun-loving people. We enjoy doing fun things. We'd rather be together and do things together than anything. Jim and I, if we had a choice of being with anybody else or by ourselves, our choice is always to do something together. After seventeen years of marriage, Jim and I are real lovers and very, very close. However, I respect Jim's privacy and he respects mine.

Even after seventeen years of marriage, I'm still embarrassed in front of Jim today. At times I still feel like a newlywed. We keep life very interesting. We tell each other we love each other every day. I don't think a night goes by but what I say to Jim, "Honey, I really love you." I love Jim more than anybody I've ever loved in the whole world.

Yes, we have our fights. We have times when we disagree violently. I'm the violent one because Jim never raises his voice. It's hard to have a one-sided argument sometimes so Jim has to be terribly, terribly upset with me before he will lift his voice.

We never go to bed mad at each other—except for the one time I have already told you about. We always get it out of our system, then it is done and it is over.

We are each other's best friend. We love the same things. We enjoy interior decorating, going out to eat, Disney World, Knott's Berry Farm, and love to take our children to carnivals and county fairs.

Jim is a very gentle and tender-hearted person. He is a very giving person. I cannot tell how much Jim has given away in our lifetime, but God has always given it back to us.

Jim has always been a person who says, "God will fight our battles."

We've had a very fantastic give-and-take marriage. I give 100% and so does Jim, so how can you lose with something like that going on between two people?

I still flirt with my husband. I tease and kid him. He teases and kids me.

I can always tell when something bothers Jim because of the expression on his face and the look in his eyes. I know when to be quiet and when to talk. There are times when Jim doesn't want to be bothered. Then there are times when I know he has to be bothered, even though he doesn't want to be.

At times I've forced the children on Jim a bit because he's really tired and likes to sit down at home, read the paper or crawl in bed and watch TV. At that time I take Jamie to him and put him in his lap and say, "Come on, honey, OUR children!" I'm not afraid to force our children on Jim. I realize they are very important to his sanity and for keeping all of life in perspective.

Jim listens to what I say. However, when he knows he has heard from God, no matter what I say won't change it. I respect that man for that because sometimes in my little womanly way I want something different than what

God wants, just because I want it.

It is an exciting life living with Jim. It is a very, very loving life. Our family is all very much in love.

We are very open with our children concerning everything. We answer their questions very frankly. We are open about sex. We feel they deserve an open, honest answer, and speak to them in terms they can understand.

I could never keep any secret from Jim because I share everything with him. Whether he's interested or not.

I love wigs and I love to look different. I can't stand to look the same way all the time. So if my hair is long, I've got to cut it short. If it's short I've got to let it grow long. I wear wigs all the time, and Jim never knows who I'm going to be. I think that's part of the fun of it. He always says, "Honey, you are one person I can't picture in my mind when I go away."

One time I walked into his office and I had just gotten a black wig. I looked like one of the Spanish girls that come for our Spanish PTL Club. Jim did not know who I was. He forbade me to ever wear that wig again. It scared him that he didn't even recognize his own wife. I laughed and laughed at him. That's the only one I've ever bought that I couldn't wear again. But it is still in my closet.

I think a wife should keep a man guessing. The fact that I'm still shy around Jim is a healthy thing because it keeps us very much in love. He tells me, "I will never figure you out. As long as I live I can't figure you out." That's one of the things he likes about me.

I always compliment Jim when he looks nice and he always compliments me. He tells me I'm the cutest and greatest woman he has ever known. I know he's fibbing, but I love it! When I wear something that he doesn't particularly care for he'll say, "Honey I don't think that's particularly flattering."

Graham, PTL Don't Abuse Trust

'et Bill Dowda (Forum, July 5) rest as-
'ed the minister who misuses money
en him for the ministry of the Gospel
ll one day forsake His riches.
Jesus warned us not to trust in riches.
en he said: "Seek ye first the kingdom
God and His righteousness and all these
ngs shall be added unto you." (Matt.
3).

know some are abusing the ministry of
gospel. But the three ministers Mr.
wda mentioned (Jim Bakker, Billy Gra-
a, Oral Roberts) seem to be sharing
irs. I receive mail every week from
L. One man cannot do it all. We are
ng into these homes; most of them are
dy, most of all they need Christ. Do
t not think John the Baptist and Christ
ald use the media? It takes money to
rate for Jesus Christ.

EUGENE BLACK
arlotte

Fund Is Shocking

/e were surprised when Katherine
ilman left an estate of over $3 million
we lifted an eyebrow at Billy Hargis.
wife and I felt the nation was dis-
:ed when Nixon accumulated two mil-
aire estates and used his crimes on TV
another million or so after resigning in
grace.

ow we are deeply shocked that Billy
ham saw fit to stash away, secretly,
million that was accumulated in Jesus'
e. Will he now follow the Watergate
onalities and write a book to further
ince his wealth? How about this for a
, "An Expose Of The Big-Time Evan-
tic Racket?" I hope he hasn't done to
tion what Nixon, Agnew and Mitchell
o the credibility of politicians.

ow many times has he preached about
a telling the young rich that if he
ted to inherit the kingdom of heaven
hould sell all he owned and give to the
?

LEE BROWN
ton, Ohio

Observer: Be Warned

iis is a gentle warning to a secular
spaper that it had better step lightly in
ng to destroy one of God's greatest
stries.

t us pray as we have never prayed be-
for any ministry, fo   'that
Graham has done in
generation. I feel tha
I know that whate
owever difficult it
I — there has to
fully satisfies God.
hall continue to p
stry in my own
beg any minister
e bandwagon of
ppraisal that they in....
s in fear and trembling.
million dollars or so in a worldwide
stry is peanuts in this inflated time.
ministry has people all over the world
converts from Hong Kong to Califor-
nd beyond.

"TAKE ALL THAT YOU HAVE AND GIVE UNTO THE POOR, AND COME, FOLLOW ME!"

(Marlette cartoon of July 3)

lavishly and acquired millions under false
pretenses and without an interest in the
souls of men.

These men are liars and deceivers. Rev
21:8 tells us that "... All liars shall ha'
their part in the lake which burneth w
fire and brimstone ...."

I hope your efforts to expose thes
ocrites continue since it provides
service to the public.

JOHN H. R
Elgin, S.C.

Overcome Temr

Billy Graham advised
er, July 6) to overcor
with scripture as Chr
11). Does Graham '
prescribes?

Let Graham te'
took to justify h'
from the poor r
ly. Was it t'
you, do '
6:31, "And
to you, do
I wish

Marlette Attack Unfair

mely doubtful that Mr. Mar-
on a soul for Jesus Christ,
 'o men he so shameles-

comfort in the
'he greatest
'ed Chris-

CHARLOTTE —   Haskin
nized accounting fir'
Sells a nationally
issued a bal
tion

Audit Declares PTL And Jim Bakker Financially Upright!

Praise the Lord

Charlotte club runs $15 million busines

'.ut cost PTL   .ie   .ent .an and Sells also re'
~40,000 it produced   .worth Jim Bakker of PTL Presi
Referri.   Personal audit declared Jim
about Billy G.   which is worth to leonly $20,000 ,1
(Julv 3) "The C   American family's worth Shock, d
                   ing the deepen press, it revealed
                   Jim's giving and God trusted .ng to
                   nature.   CKSC..   oint

To Get State License

PTL Must Tell
What It Spends

By JANE LEE LISENBY
News Staff Writer

The PTL Television Network, the
international television ministry
based in Charlotte, is going to have
to reveal what it's doing with its
money to a state licensing agency
because of a change in the state's so-
licitation law, says a North Carolina
licensing official.

Ed Edgerton, head of the solicita-
tion and licensing branch of the De-
partment of Human Resources, said
a bill that amended the state's solici-
tation law will require PTL and
other religious groups supported by
non-members to provide financial
statements both for religious and secular activities when filing applica-
tions for licenses.

PTL has come in for special attention
from Edgerton.

Edgerton asked PTL in a letter in
June to apply for a solic
cense and provide a finan
ment on its secular activi
came after Edgerton said
PTL's the Rev. Jim Bakke
money for a planned univ
home for the aged on th
late-night program bros
WRDU-TV (Channel 28) in

God Will Judge
Graham, Bakker

I refuse to add credit to the at-
tack on Mr. Graham and on PTL
in their use of money taken in or
acquired for the furthering of
the Gospel. God will judge these
men, and all other men, for how
they handle the affairs of the
witness for Jesus Christ.

DEXTER E. GREENE
Charlotte

Minister Spent

By WAYNE NICHOLAS
Observer Gastonia Bureau

The Rev. Garland Faw, a Kannapolis pastor, feels
more strongly than most people who complained about a
"PTL Club" interview with Hustler magazine Publisher
arry Flynt, who says he's a born-again Christian.

Faw borrowed $1,300 from his congregation at the
50-member nondenominational Truth Temple in Kan-
apolis and bought a ¾-page ad in Friday's Observer to
enounce the interview. The ad also will appear Monday
n The Charlotte News.

"I do feel very strongly about this — yes, air, $1,300
vorth," Faw said Friday. The 39-year-old minister earns
16,000 a year.

Faw's advertisement ran under the headline: "Por-
ography or the Bible, Either-Or — Not Both"

For Faw, the issue is simple. He doesn't believe Flynt
s a born-again Christian, so he thinks Jim Bakker's in-

Ad att
PTL's
interv

By JANE LEE
and JOHN V
News Staff

A Kannapolis m
tacked PTL's the R
a three-quarter-pag
vertisement, conde
gious talk show ho
ful use of the Bib
pornographer Larry
The Rev. Garia:
the nondenomin

"Anyone who (
tler' and believe in
sion is as gullible a
says a letter to the
6A.

Temple, said in
view today, he felt
ad because "they
mendous power
thought in this con
case where PTL in
the Bible is on the

N.C.
New I
On P

By MARY
Observer

North Car
newly amen
broad financia
gious organizat
PTL Television N
ted reports on ho
spends all its money
Eddie Knox, att
ternational Charlot
work, said Wednes
ing the constitutio
amended July 1.
contest the const
we'll probably see
the enforcement of
Jim Moss, execu
of PTL, said the te
would be willing
Supreme Court if t
ficials deem the la
al.

July 17, 1977 - Charlotte Observer

This letter was also signed by 27 others.

Unfortunately, some people are so critical they always manage to spot the hole and never see the doughnut. Christians are no exception.

One of the first things we need to do is stop labeling individuals. We should remove the inscription above sanctuary 'doors denoting our denominations and replace it with a sign simply reading: "The Church." We need to focus attention on Jesus Christ and forget our petty differences. If we think the world needs changing, why not first begin by changing ourselves?

It's mind-boggling to see how Christians openly condemn other Christians because their opinions differ. It's easy to love those who think as we do; however, the real test comes when we attempt to love those in the Body of Christ who have different opinions or doctrines.

A good example is the harsh criticism of _____ How many people have _____ ous thoughts _____ from su _____ lectin _____ loca _____ it _____

"BUT I HAVE CHOSEN YOU OUT OF THE WORLD... IF THEY HAVE PERSECUTED ME, THEY WILL ALSO PERSECUTE YOU." (ST. JOHN 15: 19,20

This cartoon, responding to a July 3 Observer cartoon by Doug Marlette, was sent to us by Bob Manzano, director of public relations for the PTL club. It's by Randy Stephens, a 19-year-old set designer for PTL.

There is a question in many minds regarding your motives.

PRESTON PARRISH
Winston-Salem

•

You would have people believe Billy Graham's crusades cost nothing. Just one crusade costs millions. He'll still get my monetary support, and every other Christian's.

If you fools printed a story of Christ's crucifixion between two thieves on the cross, it would be written to sound as if Christ met two bootleggers at an intersection.

BOB SCOTT
Albemarle

•

Those who live near Mr. Graham respect and love him, and most of us thought he was "getting rich" off his preaching. Still, he has done a lot of good, preached to millions and saved many wrecked lives _____

another story _____ arently _____ ne for _____ roup. _____ have _____ of _____ ty _____ from _____ ng the _____ PTL. I blame _____ ident — the FCC _____ state — for not stepping in and at least asking for an accounting.

ROBERT WARREN
Asheville

It will help build community pride.

there is no vision, we will perish. Char-

SAND _____

not surprised by _____
I'm ashamed of _____

It is a _____
Grah _____

Manzano said "We could improve the quality of _____ the public should _____ religious organizations _____ how _____ Law _____ is received, Law _____ audit _____ the information and send _____ verify the information on listings will _____ recommendation and _____ will _____ network will decide whether _____ office—That office will decide whether to approve the _____

I am disappointed that The Observer would stoop to muckraking and yellow journalism in its treatment of Billy Graham.

The Observer seems _____ ve lost sight of its journa _____ lte ethics by refusing to v _____ lectical story on the f _____

T PRICE

Doesn't your paper have _____ thing better to do than to _____ ear campaign about _____ Believe me, _____ e done

Officers of the PTL television _____ work Monday provided a preliminary _____ financial information to the Char- _____ lotte Better Business Bureau (BBB) _____ audit _____ tentatively promised a few days, _____ the meeting came _____ president of the Charlotte bureau, _____ said last week the Charlotte-based _____ evangelical television organization might _____ be put on the bureau's national "unap- _____ proved donations list if it did not _____ provide information on fund-raising _____

Law said a 45-minute meeting _____ Monday with PTL president and host _____ Jim Bakker and public relations di- _____ rector Robert _____ of what I need to _____ "the majority of what I need to _____ consider the network for bureau list- _____ ing.

Manzano said the network turned _____ over to Law board members, affili- _____ tion, a list of staff and their salaries, _____ ties, and staff and their salaries, _____ Methods of distributing materials _____ and soliciting money were pub- _____ mitted, Manzano said. _____ PTL will be the first major reli- _____ ous organization to be on the BBB

three years _____
would comply if asked _____
'i don't want to get in an adver- _____
sary position with PTL Club and his _____
officers," Law said Friday, but he _____
still maintained Bakker knew of the _____
correspondence. "I'd like to see the _____
audit," he said, "having disposed _____
made on it and continue on regular _____
BBB work and put PTL behind us."

From my own personal experience and visits to PTL Club, I know these people are sincere, people who love and are concerned about lost souls. There have been times that I couldn't have made it, had it not been through their prayers and faith. God did answer their prayers and mine, too. _____

"But they mocked the messengers of God, and despised his words, and misused his prophets, until the wrath of the Lord rose against his people, till there was no remedy." (II Chronicles 36:16).

Charlotte

PEGGY HAYNE _____ e Page

News

lotte and The Carolinas

---

with an unsaved pornographer, in effect, condone pornography.

r, who hosts the Charlotte-based TV program, he believes Flynt was converted. He says he ondone pornography but believes mature Christ an obligation to teach the Gospel to and love istians" like Flynt.

s simply asking people to pray for him," Bakker. "You've got to be deaf and dumb and blind not m against pornography, but the stand of the should be to love the sinner and hate the sin. way to stamp out pornography is to get every her saved."

aid he felt an obligation to speak out because People That Love" Network has "tremendous mold religious thought in the Charlotte area.

The interview was shown at 11 a.m. Monday on WRET (Channel 36) in Charlotte and was shown live or taped on 174 affiliate stations.

Faw said he thought it was impossible for Flynt to have been converted to Christianity and still publish pornography.

Flynt said he was converted just before Thanksgiving while flying on a plane with Ruth Carter Stapleton, President Carter's evangelist sister. He said it would take at least five months to change Hustler because the magazine had been printed that far in advance.

Asked about Flynt's statement, Faw said Flynt should have blocked sale of the magazine if he was a Christian.

"I've done nothing but ask prayer (for Flynt)," Bakker said. "He's a 90-day-old Christian .... Flynt admitted to me in a private conversation he doesn't have the answers yet, but that he was trying to find them.

What more can you ask of a 90-day-old baby Christian?"

The PTL host said Flynt invited his family to spend a weekend with him.

Bakker said he would like to go over Scriptures with Flynt and pray with him.

"And then I would advise him to close down Hustler and all of his other pornography magazines and papers or turn them into totally Christ-honoring publications, telling him that as a born-again Christian, he can no longer be a part of the old way of life."

Bakker said he sent a letter to Faw after seeing the ad. It read:

"Dear Garland: God bless you. I love you. I am praying for you. I trust that you will pray for me, too. Jim Bakker."

Faw said he appreciated the thoughts but added, "I do feel he (Bakker) is desperately wrong about this. I want him to publicly confess he is wrong."

Jim never downs me. He never makes me feel inferior. He has been my secret of success in anything I've ever done because He's always made me feel I could do it. I've always believed that Jim could do anything. I know that anything Jim Bakker sets his mind to do, he can do it. I've never seen him fail at anything he's put his mind to. I believe it is because we've worked together and encouraged each other and trusted in the Lord.

Jim told me I could sing and I knew I couldn't. He's always telling me, "You can do it. You are as good as anyone. Just hold your head up and you can do it, baby." If he thinks that, that's all in the world that counts to me. It makes me feel ten feet tall, even though I'm only four feet and eleven inches.

I wouldn't trade Jim for anything in the whole wide world. I believe that when Jesus created Jim and me, He made us for each other.

We've been going through some real unbelievable things lately.

Things had been going along real well at PTL when suddenly the newspapers decided that they were going to try to dig up some dirt on us and there certainly had to be some somewhere. "There's no ministry that can be as clean as the Bakker's say their ministry is." We had never had anyone question our honesty or ministry before.

People can look in our checkbook anytime they want and see how much money we have in the bank. They can look through anything personal that we have. Pat Robertson used to say that Jim Bakker would tell people what he ate for breakfast if they asked him.

When the newspapers decided they were going to see if they could dig up some dirt on us and began to question our honesty and integrity we couldn't believe it when we got wind of what was coming. We never dreamed that it was going to be as bad as it was.

We had bought a home in South Carolina where we could have some privacy. After the newspapers interviewed Jim they would tangle up everything so it came out wrong in print. They got persons that didn't like us or our ministry and wrote about it in the papers. One of the newspaper men posed as a man looking for real estate (that was the only way he could get into the subdivision where we live as there are guards at the gate). He took pictures of our home. Then went to the county records to find out how much we paid for it, how much we put down and how much money we owed. The next thing we knew our house and personal business was on the front page of the newspaper.

It got to where we had to have an audit of PTL, and one for ourselves, so that we could prove that what we said was true. All of my jewelry, and all of the things that for years we had sacrificed to buy, we had to have them appraised. All of our bank statements for several years were looked at. Someone came to the house to see how many couches, televisions, refrigerators, washers and dryers we had.

I thought I was going to die during this time. I was fighting desperately for some privacy. I thought how wrong it was to go into anybody's personal life and reveal it to the world. It wasn't fair. Some thought we were millionaires and the audit showed our worth to be $15,000.

Jim almost had another nervous breakdown. He would not go out of the house to eat, or hardly go anywhere. He would come home at night and go to bed and just lie staring at the ceiling and praying. For several weeks he did not take me out once because he couldn't stand the ridicule. Everywhere we went just about all we heard was PTL, PTL, PTL. Some were calling it "pass the loot." Jim was being called all sorts of names.

I knew how bad off Jim was because whenever he

121

starts getting nervous his stomach starts hurting him and he withdraws into himself.

One day I was in the bedroom and saw a little card on the nightstand with the following verse: "The trial of your faith is more precious than gold." That day when Jim got up and dressed, he stuck it in his pocket. When he was in the kitchen I noticed it was propped up by the sink: "The trial of your faith is more precious than gold." When I went to his office later, there was that verse again. He carried it with him and would take it out of his pocket and lay it down in front of him: "The trial of your faith is more precious than gold." That was the only way he got through the newspaper articles, which for weeks and weeks bombarded us.

All of this made me very bitter. I wanted to write a letter to the newspaper and tell them what I thought. God then spoke to me saying, "Tammy, that's not the way to do it. Let Me show you what to write the newspaper."

I sat down and began to write what God was speaking to me. "A love letter to Jim." The Holy Spirit really wrote that letter. I sent it to the newspaper. After that things began to look up. People began to look at some good sides of PTL.

There is almost nothing in the world that Jim and I hate more than pornograpny. When we heard that Larry Flynt had gotten saved and that many Christians were denouncing him, we felt he needed a friend. We knew that if he was going to make it that somebody had to help him. The issue wasn't pronography, it was that a man had been born again.

Only God knows what happened when we took Larry Flynt under our wing. Jim literally put his ministry on the line. Jim wasn't afraid. He said, "I'm not going to have the blood of this man on my hands when I stand before Jesus. If I don't help him, who is going to?"

From Tammy Bakker

A Love Letter To Jim

Tammy Bakker, the wife of the PTL Club's Jim Bakker, sent us this "love letter to my husband." The Bakkers have two children — Tammy Sue, 7, who just completed the first grade at the First Church of the Nazarene School on Scaleybark Road, and Jamie Charles, 18 months. They live in River Hills at Lake Wylie, S.C.

Dear Jim:

To one of the most kind, honest and sincere men I've ever known, I love you, honey. I've seen the awful hurt in your eyes lately as you have read this paper and have seen your good name run down by people who do not even know you. People that don't know and don't care about the sacrifices you have made and the tears I have seen you shed as you have tried to do your part to make this world a better place to live in.

I have never known you to sell anything that gives people cancer, nor to offer people drink that causes them to kill and destroy other people and the things they love. The only thing you are guilty of is offering a new, happy life to others through God!

I wish I could somehow tell you how my heart has ached for you as I've seen you work day and night, and toss and turn in your sleep, trying to figure out how to raise the millions of dollars it takes to help bring something besides sex and violence to the TV screen around this world. So many times I've wanted to scream, "Honey, it just isn't worth it."

Then, I remember what this God you preach about has done in my own life and the joy He has brought me, and suddenly it makes it all worthwhile again.

I've seen you sit for hours with supposedly honest reporters and answer their questions frankly and honestly, when I knew you really did not have the time. Then, I've seen the hurt in your eyes as you opened the newspaper and read the story they had written, and everything you said had been twisted to make better copy.

No, honey, I've never known you to throw a tantrum. How I've wished you would sometimes.

I've never heard you tell a lie, although many times it would have been the easy way out. I've never known you to cover up anything or try to hide anything. Our business life, even our personal life, has always been open to anyone who would really want to know, but then

Observer Photo By JIM WILSON

Jim And Tammy Bakker
...with Tammy Sue and Jamie

I've only lived with you 16 years. Maybe the people who are writing these letters and drawing the cartoons know you better than I do.

Love, your Wife,

Tammy

It wasn't very long ago that Larry called Ruth Stapleton saying, "Ruth, now I have two Christian friends. I have you and I have Jim Bakker."

That meant a lot to Jim Bakker. Jim said, "Give me the sinners to preach to. Somebody else can take the Christians."

The people who have treated us the worst in the ministry have been those who call themselves Christians. Sinners have never treated us real bad, and often have been the ones that come and say, "Man, we really respect you. You are doing a great job!" I put a question mark behind the word "Christian" because the Bible says the reason that you know that you've passed through death into life is because you have love one to another.

It is wonderful when God moves upon us to restore the hurts that we have caused others.

It had been years since we had seen Ralph and his wife. We were attending the Lutheran Charismatic Conference in Minneapolis. The Lord spoke to Jim, "If you are going to truly be Christian and love the world, ask Ralph to come and be on the PTL Club."

Jim knew that Ralph was doing a wonderful work for the Lord, so he scheduled Ralph to come to PTL. Today Ralph, his wife and Jim and I are wonderful, wonderful friends. Ralph apologized for what he did and was sorry. God has totally mended all that was between us. Ralph now supports PTL and pushes it very heavily in California.

Also, I praise God with what has happened in our relationship with Paul and Jan's pastor who didn't like us and who caused so much trouble. He is now a missionary on the mission field. Not long ago he wrote a letter to Jim saying, "Jim I was wrong. I was terribly wrong to do what I did to you as a Christian brother. I want to ask you to forgive me. Please, please, forgive me."

Jim wrote back, "Why sure, pastor. I forgive you.

You know I forgive you."

God has worked it all out and there's been victory plus victory. God is so faithful and His Word so sure!

Chapter 14

THE "TAMMY FAYE" SHOW

Since I've been in Christian television I've had one desire and it was to do a woman's show. God knew that I had to go through some really hard knocks to become a woman before I could deal with women and their problems. I know that many of the things that God has allowed me to go through have been for this very time to do my show.

When I heard that I was going to be able to do a ladies' show, my heart was singing inside. I felt God has given me the call to the average American woman. Not the one who has all the money and can buy all the expensive things she wants. God has called me to the lady with the little snotty-nosed kids running behind her screaming, "Mama," all day long. (What is the answer to her problems?) This calling is to the mother who would like to go to the beauty parlor just once but she either can't afford it, or she doesn't have the time. God has called me to the woman who can't have diamonds and furs and has to wear the fake ones. I'm called to the woman who doesn't have the money to buy new furniture for her home and who wants so desperately to make a nice home.

I want to show women how to decorate the home by

using contact paper, spray paint and getting the good deals in the bargain rooms at stores where Jim and I buy most of our furniture. We buy the scratched and dented stuff and make it look like a million. I want to show how one can rub peanut butter into certain furniture and you won't even see the scratch. How one can stain things with shoe polish. How one can create and be proud of what you have done. So that when people say, "Oh, what a nice home you have," you can say, "This was an old outdoor statue that I sprayed gold and rubbed it down in antiquing solution. I only paid $5 for it."

I want to show women how they can dress and look great by getting one simple black outfit, and by adding a scarf, a vest, a blouse here and there and have many outfits.

How by taking a few strands of costume jewelry, that cost a dollar or two, and placed in the right spot can look very sharp.

How to buy an inexpensive wig for when you can't get to the beauty parlor.

How one can buy the right pair of shoes and one good pair of boots and they'll look good with anything one puts on.

I'm doing this show primarily for the woman who doesn't know Jesus and needs an answer.

We're going to show the average American woman how she can make her face look beautiful even though she feels insecure. How she can be beautiful by applying just the right amount of make-up. And where she can go to buy this make-up from $1 to $4. She can look as pretty as the woman who pays $20 a bottle for her make-up. I've done it all of my life. I feel God has shown me how.

We are going to discuss problems like smoking, drinking, breast cancer, and anything else that concerns women. We are going to talk about the woman who gets up in the morning and has to have a drink. We will discuss it as it is.

So what if there isn't an answer? We'll admit we don't know what the answer is. But there is Someone who can tell us the answer: Jesus Christ. There is always an answer in Jesus. We might not have it ourselves, but if you come to know Jesus as your personal Saviour, we'll get an answer for you. I'll guarantee it.

I'm excited and praising God every day that He is allowing me to do this.

Chapter 15

RHINESTONE CHRISTIAN

I have always hated pride, and I know God also hates pride. Pride is one of the things that hurts me most about people that God has chosen to use for His glory. You see them in the pulpit, on TV, or in crusades as dedicated people who love the Lord. You hear them singing or preaching with tears streaming down their faces asking souls to come to Jesus, then after the meeting, etc., you see them turn into proud people who won't give someone who is "below them" the time of day.

I have every opportunity to watch and be with these people. I have never felt comfortable around them. And believe me, I wouldn't be around them at all, if it weren't for my particular station in life—the wife of the President of PTL.

How many times have I seen them trying to out-perform, out-dress and out-accomplish each other. All in the name of Jesus. I have many times seen them push and shove and hurt each other trying to get ahead. I wonder so often if they are doing God's work or simply working for themselves, using God as a cheap method into show business.

There have been those come to PTL and refuse to sing

because our equipment wouldn't make them sound good enough. Who are they doing it for, themselves or Jesus? Are they not willing to fail if they have to for the Lord? By fail I mean be less than perfect if an opportunity to minister presents itself and if it means winning a soul. It might even mean singing without any equipment whatsoever!

I believe in giving the very best to Jesus. I also believe in professionalism, but what if someone needs help and we don't have our professional tracks with us? Do we refuse to minister . . . or if the sound system isn't the best, do we refuse to minister for Him?

Many now come to PTL and fall all over us. However, before PTL became an instrument for God they wouldn't give Jim or I the time of day. How I abhor this kind of behavior, and I am certain the Lord does also.

Then there are the so-called Christian cliques! If you're not in, you're just not in! I recently went to a Christian convention and what I saw there turned my stomach. It was like a Far Eastern bazaar. I stood there and watched people playing the game! I saw the hurt eyes of outsiders, and, yes, felt hurt myself as certain people made believe I really wasn't standing 5 feet away from them. I just wasn't there in their so-called "class." I wasn't a song writer, I wasn't a singer with a number one album. I just didn't count in their eyes. I felt their coldness toward me, yet their overwhelming warmth to the people that could further their careers. Would I have been the one receiving all the attention if I could further their career? I wonder. I trust that I wouldn't desire it or even want it! Perhaps it is just a human failure. I know that I also have days when I let the pressure of answering questions, saying "hello" a thousand times, that I, too, perhaps seem aloof and distant. *Please God, help me keep under the blood. I don't want to be that way ever.*

There are some artists I truly admire. One is Norma Zimmer, I'll never forget the day I met Norma. I was afraid. But I met a fantastic lady, a lady who was just exactly the way I saw her on TV. Sweet and lovely and very kind. She has time for everyone, even our cameramen. That is one way I can tell much about the people that come to PTL. If they are as nice to the cameramen, as they are to Jim and I, that says something to me.

I love Hank Snow. He is a real person! Jim Hampton is another real person. Gary S. Paxton . . . who has a better right to be proud because of all his accomplishments? But his humble spirit has endeared him to millions of TV viewers. C. M. Ward—fantastic, in my book. The Blackwood Brothers, Dale Evans, Little Richard, Senator Mark Hatfield, Judge Kermit Bradford, Carol Lawrence, Maude Aimee and Rex Humbard, Dean Jones, Art Linkletter, Robert Schuller, all fantastic, real people. Jerry Clower, Oral and Evelyn Roberts, the Singing Speers, Jeanie C. Riley, Stu Phillips, Stewart Hamblin, The Rambos, The Flying Wallendas team, Lu Lu Roman, Charles Colson, and Andrew Caulverwell are all great people of God.

I know that the world also is fighting to get to the top hurting one another, but Christians are supposed to be different. We are supposed to love, to treat each other as equals, and, yes, to even prefer our brothers. We are to be the light of the world. What is happening today to Christians? Have we all forgotten our real purpose? "PLEASE GOD HELP US!"

Chapter 16

I GOTTA BE ME

Pride and jealousy are two of Satan's greatest tools that he uses against God's children. We must be constantly on the alert against them.

Recently, at PTL a couple of the men were treating Jim badly. He was just about to break under the strain of it. What hurts Jim, hurts me twice as bad. We were sitting on the bed one night and Jim looked at me in despair and said, "Tammy, what am I going to do?"

I was ready to get on the phone and tell the men to "you know what" because I was so frustrated and so angry at what they were doing to my husband, and the things they were putting on him that he could not take, could not handle and didn't need.

God gave me an object lesson through the song of the telephone company commercial: "Let Your Fingers Do the Walking Through the Yellow Pages." He showed me the yellow pages and the fingers walking over them. "Tammy, that is the way I want you to pray. I want your prayers to do your walking for you," God spoke. "That way you won't make a mistake and blow the whole roof off of PTL."

I shared this with Jim and we both decided to let our

prayers do the walking for both of us.

Time and time again, things have gone wrong, people have hurt us and Jim would be in a situation where I couldn't do anything but pray. Then I would see God undertake and deliver. My prayers were doing the walking for me. Prayer really works!

Whatever the problem was at the time, God took care of it. But I made up my mind that it was not going to happen again. Never again was I going to allow anyone to take away anything from the man I love, Jim Bakker. If we had not gone through the California experience it could have happened in Charlotte. Even today, when something arises at PTL that isn't just what it should be, I once again feel threatened, because I know Jim wouldn't fight for it.

Maybe some day God will say, "You are through here," but I believe we are living in the last days and I doubt that God will ever make us build a ministry from scratch again. But we are willing if it should ever come to that!

The California experiences caused me to be very suspicious of people, even the people that I dearly love. It has caused me to have something in my heart. I pray that it will go away, but it's still there. The very first thoughts that come into my heart when new people come into our organization are, "Is that the one? Is he going to try to take over now? Is he going to start something this time? Is he going to cause a rustling?"

I never know who is my real friend. This is one of the problems of being well-known. Who is your real friend? Are they the ones who are saying, "I love you" just because I am Tammy and not for what they can get from me? Are they the ones who say, "I'm just going to hang on her coattail and see what she can do for me. I'll make her think that I love her. But if she can't do anything for me I'll drop her." The Bible says the Spirit will witness in our hearts, and that's why I always try to keep a tender and humble spirit before the Lord, because I need to know I have friends.

I have one true girl friend, Linda Wilson. I know I can tell her anything. She loves me because she knows I'm me. She doesn't love me because of PTL, or that I can do something for her. She'd love me if the whole thing fell apart and we didn't have a thing tomorrow. Linda and I would still stick together. We pray together. We cry together. We laugh together and we express our fears together. I tell things to Linda that I can't tell anyone else. My husband doesn't understand sometimes because it's "girl talk."

I'm still suspicious of people who come and are "buddy buddy" around Jim. If my spirit doesn't bear witness with them I say, "Honey, don't let them smother you. Be sensitive to God." When people come that we are to hire I tell Jim, "Be careful, be sensitive. Let's pray about it. Be careful because you won't know unless God speaks to your heart."

Sometimes I almost resent new people who come into our organization. It's all butter for them. Many of us have cried, pinched pennies and sacrificed. Now most come in expecting a big salary, fine office and equipment, etc., and they haven't had to go through anything to get to this point. Many of the people take it all so for granted. It breaks my heart. I want to say to them, "Don't you know blood, sweat, prayers and tears have been shed for this ministry? Can't you understand that there was a price paid to get this ministry where it is today? Can't you understand the sacrifices of our partners to keep this ministry on the air? Don't you realize this is a ministry and not just a business?"

I have always felt if people aren't called to the ministry they shouldn't be working at PTL. If they don't have that burning desire to see souls saved then they are in the wrong place. But it is so hard to find 700 other people that care as much as we do. However, I really feel that most of our staff at PTL do care.

We have many people in our ministry who are very loyal and have stood with us over the long haul. They know the value of receiving and giving. The same is also true of many of the guests who appear on the show. Many of them are unaware of the cost that was required to build this place. They perform, take their honorariums and leave, hoping it has helped further their career. This breaks my heart.

Dino and Debbie Kartsonakis were scheduled to come to be on the PTL Club. I was so excited for I believe he is the greatest Christian pianist I have ever heard. He was with Kathryn Kuhlman, and when she died that left Dino without a platform. When they arrived I thought: "They have just come to hang on our coattails to see if we can help their career and make them more popular."

The first thing they came up with was, "We want to do a variety show."

Sure, that's what it is. "They want to do a variety show and want PTL to foot the bill," I thought.

I wanted to love them. I wanted to say, "Dino and Debbie, you are my friends and I love you." However, I couldn't say that because I really didn't know. I distrusted Debbie because I thought she couldn't possibly love someone like me. She is beautiful and has had so many lovely things and all the riches of life I never had. She had been in Las Vegas. She had been a show girl. Why, she couldn't possibly like someone from South International Falls, Minnesota, who had an outdoor bathroom! I said to Linda, "They have got to be here because of television and what it can do for them."

(Dino and Debbie are now scheduled to be on PTL

once a month.) As each time for their appearance on the program drew near my heart would react the same way. Fear and insecurity would begin to flood over me once again. The time came for their visit. I made myself scarce hoping that I wouldn't have to see Debbie. I had just gone to the beauty parlor that day and had my hair colored and styled. I felt a total wreck because it didn't turn out.

Jim and I were at home. I was in my faded, old robe. I was all upset because of my hair, when a knock came on the door. Jim opened the door. There stood Dino and Debbie. Tears sprang into my eyes and I ran for the bedroom, determined I would not come out until they left. I was also praying that Jim would come up with a good excuse for me and that they would leave. After a half hour it became evident that Jim wasn't going to do a thing for me. I knew I had to be polite and come out of the bedroom and keep up the good front as Jim's wife and face them.

I changed my clothes and walked into the living room to face Debbie's hugs and kisses.

The Kartsonakis' were on their way to the TV studio to view the finished product of their "variety show" and begged us to go along. We did! And me, terribly miserable the whole time.

Never, to my knowledge, did Debbie ever suspect how I really felt. I always held my head high around her—even though my heart was in my throat.

Debbie and Dino had been talking about me, and God must have given them an insight into what I was really feeling. I will never forget the day. I was standing on the set of my new show when Debbie walked up to me, took ahold of my hand, and slipped a beautiful diamond ring on my finger. She then said, "Tammy, I really do love you!"

I could not say a word. I was speechless. Tears ran

down my face as I looked into Debbie's eyes. All I could say was, "Debbie, you will never know what this ring means to me. Someday I will tell you the whole story." I knew that Debbie loved that ring because she was wearing it herself and had gotten it for Christmas.

That event was God's way of saying, "Tammy, I care about your feelings, and I am showing you in a way which you will understand that Debbie and Dino are for real and really do love you. They love you just because you are you, and not for what you, Jim, or PTL can do for them."

Now all of the suspicion in my heart is gone and I know that Debbie loves me just because I'm me. I know if PTL fell apart that Dino and Debbie would still be friends of Jim and Tammy Bakker.

Nobody knows what it's like to be in the limelight, unless they have been there themselves. I know how much one wants to be just a person like everyone else, and not be set on a pedestal, and not have to live up to something all the time that you really aren't.

Jim told me one day, tears streaming down his face, "Honey, do you realize that you are the only friend I have?"

Since then Roger Wilson, Roger Flessing and his wife Kathy have come into our lives. They know we have as many bad points as anyone. They know our failings and they know our successes. They know our weaknesses and they know our strengths and yet still love us. That is a true friendship. A true friend is more precious than gold! Oh, for a true friend.

I said to Linda, "So help me, if you ever leave me as your friend, I don't know what I'll ever do." You have to have that one person you can trust, that one person that you can scream and yell at and they still love you. Linda knows I scream at my kids, but she doesn't think I love Jesus any less. I think we need to quit trying to be perfect.

People need to accept people as they are, not try to change them. Linda doesn't try to change me because she knows I gotta be me! Jim doesn't try to change me because he knows I gotta be me. He loves me when my armor streaks. He loves me with my failings just as much as he loves me when I do good things.

I've told Jim many times: "One of these days I'm going to jump out and be totally me, regardless of what anybody says—I'm going to be me." I have started doing that lately on TV. If the audience doesn't like me, it is okay, but I gotta be me. If I want to giggle, I'm going to giggle. If I want to cry, I'm going to cry. I'm what Jesus made me. That's why I had to call this book *I Gotta Be Me*.